UNIFICATION
OF SOCIAL WORK

UNIFICATION OF SOCIAL WORK

Rethinking Social Transformation

Brij Mohan

Foreword by Leon H. Ginsberg

PRAEGER

Westport, Connecticut
London

Library of Congress Cataloging-in-Publication Data

Mohan, Brij, 1939–
    Unification of social work : rethinking social transformation /
    Brij Mohan ; foreword by Leon H. Ginsberg.
       p.   cm.
    Includes bibliographical references and index.
    ISBN 0–275–96114–1 (alk. paper)
    1. Social service—Sociological aspects. 2. Sociology.
    I. Title.
    HV40.M562 1999
    361.3'2—DC21   99–22110

British Library Cataloguing in Publication Data is available.

Library of Congress Catalog Card Number: 99–22110
ISBN: 0–275–96114–1

First published in 1999

Praeger Publishers, 88 Post Road West, Westport, CT 06881
An imprint of Greenwood Publishing Group, Inc.
www.praeger.com

Printed in the United States of America

The paper used in this book complies with the
Permanent Paper Standard issued by the National
Information Standards Organization (Z39.48–1984).

10 9 8 7 6 5 4 3 2 1

Copyright Acknowledgments

The author and publisher gratefully acknowledge permission to reprint the following
material written by Brij Mohan: "The Professional Quest for Truth" and "Self, Society, and Science" from the *International Journal of Contemporary Sociology*; "Toward
New Global Development" from *International Social Work*, granted by International
Social Work and Sage Publications; and "Social Work: The End or a New Beginning?" from the *Indian Journal of Social Work* of the Tata Institute of Social Sciences.

For
my students
who helped me learn
the meaning of discourse

"There are no moral phenomena at all, but only a moral interpretation of phenomena."

—Friedrich W. Nietzsche (1966: 85)

"Where the mind is without fear and the head is held high;
  Where knowledge is free; . . .
  Where the clear stream of reason has not lost its way into the
    dreary desert sand of old habit;
  Where the mind is led forward by thee into ever-widening
    thought and action—
  Into that heaven of freedom, my Father, let my country
    awake."

—Rabindranath Tagore ([1941] 1993: xxxv, 13)

Contents

Foreword

In his *Unification of Social Work*, Brij Mohan continues his complex and philosophical analyses of current social issues, especially those facing his profession, social work. His essays on the human condition and his intellectual efforts to explain social work's functioning and its alternatives have, for more than a decade, provided a stimulating and provocative basis for social work's efforts to understand and explain itself.

This latest work follows in a great social work tradition in which some of its key leaders also serve as its greatest critics. Scholars as diverse as the late Scott Briar and the late Harry Specht along with many long-time and frequent contributors to the intellectual base of the profession have, since the 1950s, questioned the premises under which social work operates and proposed new solutions or syntheses that may rationalize and improve the profession to which, like Mohan, they have dedicated their professional lives. Writers such as Mark Courtney of the University of California, Berkeley, Joel Fischer of the University of Hawaii, Duncan Lindsey of the University of California at Los Angeles, David Stoesz of Virginia Commonwealth University, and many others, have expressed their devotion to social work by pointing to its shortcomings and the trends in its development. Brij Mohan is in that tradition and *Unification of Social Work* is the latest of many friendly and concerned critiques of the social work profession.

Mohan provides a bridge between these internal critics and the writings of current and classic, more general social philosophers such as Michel Foucalt, Erich Fromm, Francis Fukuyama, Immanuel Kant, Soren Kierkegaard, Jean Paul Sartre, Jurgen Habermas, Christopher Lasch, Herbert Marcuse, C. Wright Mills, and many others whose work is cited and explicated in this remarkable essay.

Of course, social work is a different sort of profession and its critics may be too harsh for a discipline that is, essentially, a product of the contemporary society, whatever the times. Social work does what its supporters and financiers assign it. If it were self-sufficient, it might function more closely to the ways its critics, including Mohan, would like. However, it only survives by doing what it is hired to do—more like public school teachers, police officers, and institution managers— than like the more independent professions of law and medicine. Of course, it can influence what society expects of it, and works such as this one are examples of the ways in which that influence is formulated and exercised.

But the arguments about the virtues and shortcomings of social work will continue. They constitute important issues for the students of the profession and those who teach them. One hopes that students and teachers of social work, as well as its practitioners, will read this book and other critiques of the profession. It is only through studying and understanding arguments such as Mohan's that the profession will continuously deal with its internal and external criticisms and more effectively deal with them.

Leon H. Ginsberg

Preface

When a reality of human existence has completed its historical course, has been shipwrecked and lies dead, the waves throw it up on the shores of rhetoric, where the corpse remains for a long time. Rhetoric is the cemetery of human realities, or at any rate a Home for the Aged. The reality itself is survived by its name, which, though only a word, is after all at least a word and preserves something of its magic power.

—Jose Ortega y Gasset ([1932] 1957: 116–117)

Interdisciplinarity, its politics and ethics, assumed a special role in the post-Enlightenment era that fostered the rise and fall of departmentalized education. On the heels of the Enlightenment, nineteenth-century civilization produced a hybrid of liberal democracy and technicism, which, according to Jose Ortega y Gasset (1957: 107–114), represented the phenomenon of the "mass-man." The actual "scientific man," Ortega contends, is the prototype of the mass-man:

Not by chance, not through the individual failings of each particular man of science, but because of science itself—the root of our civilization—automatically converts him into mass-man, makes him a primitive, a modern barbarian. . . . But if the specialist is ignorant of the inner philosophy of the science he cultivates, he is much more radically ignorant of the historical conditions requisite for its continuation; that is to say: how society and the heart of man are to be organized in order that there may continue to be investigators. (Ortega, 1957: 109, 114)

The paradox of Enlightenment has created islands of knowledge that represent fractured realities. The post-industrial explosion of technological advancement has further confounded this distorted human reality. Strides of meta-information alone have created a "cybertribal" schizophrenic reality that calls for the reinvention of science, values, and relationships (Mohan, 1997: 18).

At the time of writing this prefatory note, the world was aggrieving the deaths of two important celebrities—the Princess of Wales in London and Mother Teresa in Calcutta. I was particularly touched by the tide of respect and love that a sari-clad small woman evoked in the hearts of the peoples beyond the City of Joy. "Let every action of mine be something beautiful for God," said Agnes Gonxha Bojaxhiu, the woman who became the undaunting champion—a living goddess—of the lowest of the low.

"People think we are social workers," she once told a spiritual advisor. "We are not. We serve Jesus. I serve Jesus 24 hours a day" (Bhaumik, Ganguly, and McGirk, 1997: 78–84). An unabashed crusader of human dignity sought perpetual joy in soothing the wounds of the most miserable people in the gutters of Calcutta. Raising orphans in Calcutta, feeding hungry street people in Rome, and caring for babies with AIDS in Washington may constitute the main plank of international social development of which social work is increasingly becoming cognizant. Yet she disclaimed the category of "social workers." Mother Teresa, as a true believer, served her God as "a pencil in His hands."

Is social work a moral equivalent of a God-given "pencil"? Perhaps not. Social workers serve their "client" populations as catalysts of change performing a host of roles at different levels within and beyond a system. Believers of the divine faith do not think of changing the system. Mother Teresa did not even question the sources of pervasive poverty and injustice. She unconditionally gave of her love to the poorest of the people. While many target populations of the Missionaries of Charity and professional social workers as the same, the two hold fundamentally different perspectives on the human condition.

Caring and sharing nurture a civil-responsible order. Modern social

workers have scientific knowledge and tools to alleviate social problems. As specialists they perform complex functions offering problem/
population-specific services in a host of settings. They follow both
the medical and legal professional models to fashion their practice.
As practitioners, rather than charity missionaries, they seek to pro-
fessionalize the whole problem-solving process. How well do they do
in their practice? Educationally well equipped, they seem to thrive
both socially and materially within communities of people with varied
expectations and value systems. Mother Teresa would be offended if
branded as a social worker practicing with such diverse clientele in
complex settings. Yet, no social work practitioner has ever proved to
be that effective and authentic as Mother Teresa has in terms of her
service to the most needy people. After all, modern social work does
owe its origins to the philanthropic ideals of the Judeo-Christian
ethics.

Social services are social work's domain as are all social programs
that deal with poverty, disease, and suffering. Commitment to one's
calling, spiritual or professional, is the cornerstone to effectiveness
which is a legitimization imperative. While no one questions the validity of a belief system, professional legitimacy is open to public
scrutiny in the realm of scientific practice. Neither law nor medicine
is exact science. Most professionals, however, strive for this legitimacy
and achieve a measure of success on the basis of demonstrated credibility. "Soft professions" still remain in a quasi-professional category.
Social work's quest for this status is a continuing saga of identity,
confidence, and authenticity. Elements of this tripartite crisis evoke
old and new ontological issues about the "Being" of social work.

As an art and science of a problem solving profession, modern
social work has emerged as a seamless quilt of varied interventive
modalities. The stray disjunction between rhetorical semantic cants—
diversity, self determination, and social justice on one hand and vocabularies of medicalized behaviors on the contrary—have stymied
the viability of a functional smorgasbord that would otherwise represent a unified profession. What exactly do we do?—which others
cannot do—remains an unanswered question despite our ten decades
of debates.

The science of social work is an oxymoron. While reason is a primal basis for any professional help, experimental exactitude may not
be the ultimate test of scientific credibility. Morality has been the
basis of all great movements. A time has come when a global crusade

must be launched against the forces of reaction in all facets of life especially those relating to education and the human condition. I strongly believe there is an axiological rationale for this approach. At the core is the love for humanity. Carl Sagan, a man of science, didn't want prayers; he wanted proof. Reverend Joan Brown Campbell asked him, "Carl do you believe in love?" "Of course I do," he replied. "Can you prove love exists?" asked Campbell. And at first he said, "Well, certainly," but eventually he agreed that love, like faith, has something unprovable at its core, but that doesn't mean it doesn't exist (Alder, 1997: 64–65). Social workers need not prove the need for justice and equality (ubiquity of injustice and inequality is pervasive). The call for a new social work is legitimized by our collective failure to deal with unfreedom with a sense of responsibility. Social work is about transformation of human reality: from unfreedom to freedom. Merely democratic infrastructure is not enough; introspective artifice alone will not do; what is needed is freedom from global oppression (Mohan, 1985; 1985a; 1993).

Despite phenomenal philanthropic altruism, the horrors of poverty, and deprivation continue to dehumanize the oppressed people. It would be naïve of us to believe that a global army of missionaries and social workers will reform the forces of massive social injustice. Self-critical social scientists have questioned the ideology and methods of their scientific inquiry. In social work the Flexner myth has continually sustained a heated debate on the subject. While a group of over-confident practitioners have chosen to find comfort in their self-acclaimed success, critical thinkers in the profession continue to question the mission, method, and mythologies surrounding the notions of help, service, and professional excellence.

The main burden of this book is to demystify the cult of a practice that lacks validity and authenticity. Social work's ontology is posited on the balance of certain mandates: distributive justice, quality of life, and optimum freedom. We have not yet reached our Jordan. We remain a hopelessly fragmented diverse group uncommitted to our mission: social equality, justice, and freedom. We practice a mythology of denial; unless there is a universal acceptance of the fact that much of human oppression is a product of social injustice, none of our methodologies and/or programs is going to succeed. Politically expedient piecemeal scenarios of change and reform wield counterproductive results. Social work academies have yet to recognize their primary role in developing knowledge that will raise consciousness for discursive change and liberation. De-developmental programs perpetuate the shaky foundation of a soft profession that lacks both legitimacy and authenticity.

Contemporary social work is a mirror rather than a candle. Social dysfunctionalities abound in the organization and delivery of our educational system. While a total societal transformation may be beyond the prowess of the entire professional community, we can at least look ourselves in the mirror. I am not one of those who have declared the "end of social work." The logic of my work is premised on a discursive formulation that calls for a new social work (Mohan, 1996b).

"The essence of Western culture is the Magna Carta, not the Magna Mac," writes Samuel Huntington (1996: 29). Modern social work, like the West, is unique but not universal. Its application in diverse situations without "universal" elements amounts adherence to the Coca-Colonization thesis (Huntington, 1996: 28–46). Human-social reality calls for a unified discipline that is inherently consistent and applicable without conceptual contradictions and material counter-productivity. My concept of science implies a theoretical base for the applied science of aesthetico-ideological transformation of human reality. A unifying science of human nature is not a new invention, however (Fromm, 1947: 23).

In the face of daunting human misery—from genocide to poverty—one cannot escape the failure of science in liberating the oppressed people. It can be argued that knowledge as a powerful tool, without axiological constrains, can itself become a source of problem. If so, each profession ought to indulge in self-reflection and see if they have actually measured up to the goals they had established for themselves. Achieving an accreditation is one thing; performing, as a vehicle of social transformation, is another. It seems that a kind of scientific devolution is underway, or else, how could one account for massive poverty and hunger at the dawn of the twenty-first century? The call for a new social work is in order.

Unification of Social Work is a prequel to a new trilogy on *The Sociology of Social Work*. My social work career as a graduate student began among the premier cohorts of a newly founded Institute of Social Sciences, Agra University, Agra, India. After graduating from ISS, Agra in 1960, I joined India's (perhaps Asia's) first doctoral program in social work at Lucknow University. During the last four decades I have learned a great deal about human behavior, public and social policy, social work education, administration, practice, and research. I also have learned about institutional culture and human banality that promote and/or thwart people and their careers for reasons that are seldom scientific or organizationally valid. On both sides of the Atlantic (or the Pacific), there are men and women whose agendum and interests interface elements of dysfunctional culture and the politics of expedience. Ignoring this reality will amount to an evasive, self-delusional exercise.

The progress that social work has made as a profession is both impressive and remarkable. Yet, I feel genuinely concerned about certain aspects of the professional culture that I find worrisome for the future of our profession. A new fundamentalism seems to eclipse our rational faculties that are otherwise conducive to a secular theodicy. In the chapters that follow, I have spelled out my observations, experiences, and analyses about crucial facets of the profession. I don't expect an instant and overwhelming response. On my part, remaining quiet at this point in life will amount to an act of bad faith. I feel passionately about issues that are decisive for my calling.

I deeply owe an unfathomable measure of gratitude to my students, friends, and family who have buoyed my spirit to undertake work of this magnitude. Textual imperfections simply reflect my own limitations. I am grateful to *International Social Work* (Francis J. Turner & Sage), *International Journal of Contemporary Sociology* (Raj P. Mohan), and *Indian Journal of Social Work* (Partha N. Mukherji) for their permission to allow me the use of four of my articles that mainly represent Chapters Two, Three, Six, and Eight of this book. I am deeply indebted to Dr. Leon Ginsberg for his thoughtful foreword.

PART I

THE ONTOLOGY OF A PROFESSION

"Complete rational knowledge is possible only of things. [Human] is not a thing. [S/he] cannot be dissected without being destroyed."

—Erich Fromm (1957: 10)

Social work as a profession has come of age. Yet, its authenticity, effectiveness, and legitimacy continue to be at the center of discourse. The chapters presented in Part I explore the being and "otherness" of social work: professional identity; theoretical-epistemological basis for transforming social reality; quest for truth; and its paradigmatic nature.

1

The Other Profession

Among the many legacies for which the closing century of professional social work will be remembered, one will certainly be progress in our system of educational programs. Yet, as we enter the 21st century, we face two imperatives in particular: our programs must be relevant, and our graduates must be able to meet societal needs. The imperatives portend for social work education a time of reexamination to assure that we are not out of sync with realities of modern economic, social, and political life. . . . *If we do not invent our future for social work education and the profession, others will invent the future for us.*
— Barbara W. White (1998; emphasis added)

"A profession of many faces" (Morales and Sheafor, [1977] 1992) encompasses an encyclopedic range of issues. Shanti Khinduka once likened social work's mystique to a Mona Lisa smile (Khinduka, 1965: 1). The transformation of "a comprehensive helping profession" (Morales and Sheafor, 1977) from a voluntary human endeavor to a complex modern specialty is a fascinating journey. It is the story of a relatively new profession that is endowed with humankind's most primordial benevolent impulse: altruism.

The culture of caring and sharing is an aesthetico-axiological imperative of a responsible society. Many people need help for various reasons; some people are in a position to offer help for varied reasons. When help is unavailable and/or inadequate, surrogate helpers assume different roles. The implied aphorism is a simplified version of a very complex whole.

The evolution of social work as a profession is a triumph of human ingenuity and benevolence. Also, it is a response of the articulate and thoughtful in a community otherwise insensitive to the old and emerging issues that demand attention and solutions. This need-triggered, remedial problem-solving process over the centuries has gained public legitimacy. The emergence of social services and reforms as institutional provisions may be a recent development but society as a whole has been responsive to the unfulfilled needs of the people since times immemorial. A welfare society precedes the welfare state.

Unscientific notions of the causes of personal and social problems, however, have plagued societal and communal responsiveness. Dole and charity may be essential elements of a benevolent faith or creed. Philanthropic responses, howsoever benign, seldom provide adequate and unqualified help. Often do they perpetuate misery under the guise of an altruistic gesture. The failure of such measures impelled society to come up with more responsible institutional alternatives in terms of prevention, treatment, and rehabilitation—a paradigm that continues as the guiding framework of the whole social service system under the aegis of the Welfare State.

Professionalization of care, help, services—a post-war development—brought about institutional arrangements in different fields for varied unfulfilled needs and exigencies. It is an irony that evils of war also generated public support for social services and professional help. In many ways, many social service systems that improved the quality of life are owed to the necessities highlighted by the horrors of the world wars. Scientific knowledge and advancements reinforced the need and provision of professional help. A problem-solving process and method eventually evolved into a professional enterprise. Sufferers and victims became clients; workers and providers assumed differential practitioners' roles. Schools and colleges offered courses and curricula imparting education and training equipping the new professionals with specialized knowledge, skills, and values. The emergence of a new breed of educated professionals who helped individuals, groups, and communities with scientific knowledge thus represented a cultural advancement in the realm of human-social problems. However, the effectiveness of such scientific endeavors continues to baffle scientists despite a scientific revolution. In addition, the legitimacy and authenticity aspects further deepen the common concerns of professional effectiveness.

If we have been able to walk on the moon and cure polio, tuberculosis, and plague, why have we failed as a responsible society to eradicate violence, poverty, and squalor from the face of this earth? The staggering progress of technology and science has unleashed a specter of knowledge. Yet our ignorance about the basic issues betrays any reasonable answer. Our scientific treatises often quantify the obvious and "practitioners" continue to "practice" without knowing much about the mystifying dynamics of social misery. A paradox of professional advancement and enlightened superstitions and continuing social malaise remains a staggering challenge to all those who intend to eradicate misery and malaise from this planet. The chapters that follow offer a perspective on the failures of a loftier instinctual response gone awry.

The dynamics of unselfish behavior is intriguing and complex. The evolution of altruism has emanated from certain Darwinian trappings that we instinctually employ in self-perpetuating interests. *Unfaithful Angels* (Specht and Courtney, 1994) is a conceited self-congratulatory metaphor. One could arguably substitute it by "faithful survivors" which explains the duality of our egoism and careerism in an exceedingly competitive world.

PROFESSION X

Conceptions of social work, like an enigmatic specter, vary from person to person. Even though professional literature abounds in definitions, social work's nature and scope remain elusive beyond the professional circles. Among professionals, conceptions vary on a wide range of ideological spectrum. The public perception is usually more benign but less articulate. It is not uncommon to find the next door person asking illiterate yet difficult questions about our calling. When I say, "I teach social work," the other person—who is not always a social worker—usually retorts: "You mean social science." Expressions betraying a reasonable understanding abound in different cultures.

Michael Mandelbaum, a former presidential advisor, of the Johns Hopkins School of Advanced International Studies describes Clinton's foreign policy as "social work" (Kondracke, 1998: 7B). The continuing debate amongst social workers about what constitutes real social work is both puzzling and mystifying. I recently wrote an article on certain conceptual-epistemological issues (Mohan, 1996a) which was rejected by two establishment journals on grounds that it was not social work. Rejection of an article is not an issue here. The reviewers' shocking intolerance of theoretical issues and shallow knowledge of the subject, their absolute arbitrary authority, and the professional license that is granted to them at members' and contributors' expense speak volumes about the exclusionary state of a calling that we all serve as diverse professionals. Professions are the new citadels of a post-modern society where hierarchical power is acquired not earned. The fact that only Darwinians win is not that unsettling; what is most worrisome is that there are no rules in the game.

A few years ago I was about to give a lecture in a required social policy course on Reaganomics and its impact on social work. An angry young man walked out of my class in protest saying that the subject had nothing to do with social work. As a social policy instructor, like many others in this field, I encountered resistance, put mildly, to policy as a discipline. As a dean, a popular fellow colleague threatened me with lawsuits if I required publications as a requirement for promotion and tenure. Social workers continue to detest serious analysis, research, and scholarly pursuits because these professional obligations, in their minds, do not relate to social work practice. The student who walked away from my social policy discourse and the esteemed colleague who threatened me with a lawsuit if I required him to produce research represent a dominant old tradition in social work which has, without offering scientific justification, elevated the practitioners' role to a cult. Dissidents in this community of faithfuls are declared pariahs. Truth is lynched in the temples of learning.

Context and contents are mutually productive constructs. It is difficult to comprehend a professional culture completely independent of the social climate of the community it serves. Post-industrial affluence and global economy have shattered national boundaries. A new work ethic is developing that is deeply rooted in the cultural crisis of our generation. One can hypothesize that deflation of ideals has promoted a self-centered post-individualism that thrives on its unprincipled success. I will argue that corruption of institutional culture is the genesis of the crisis of social work.

The motif of Generation X is a fearless pursuit of power. Money is only a vehicle in this universal quest. What makes Generation Xers unique in their unabashed competitiveness is a guilt-free adherence to acquisitive impulses. They are both secular and selfish unlike their predecessors who worshipped a feudal ideology of hereditary entitlements. The new cult of material success is therefore modern and tribal at the same time. Most believe "I have to take what I can get in this world because no one is going to give me anything" (Hornblower, 1997: 62). These x-citing, x-pansive, go-getters have revived the new material ethic which proclaims that "the only meaningful measure of success is money" (Hornblower, 1997: 66).

The consumers of our produce—expertise in a problem-solving arena—are hedonist seekers of a short cut to self-inflicted pain. Monica Lewinsky suffered a loss of libido and she needed a therapist! In a culture where instant gratification has substituted religion, painkillers, and Band-Aids come handy as fixers. While our "curriculum wars" (Katz, 1997: 53) diminish the impact of holistic learning, our professionals wallow in the newly found Jordan. The higher the fees, the better and quicker is the relief. No wonder in this intoxicated milieu, the real issues that plague the society never raise their ugly heads.

Elitist schools of social work, charging as much as $25,000 for tuition, design their curriculum with lofty ideals of diversity and social justice. A fellow dean tells me about his school which runs purely on entrepreneurial basis. His students are not asking questions about thermonuclear war; they have little knowledge about Rwanda; they have no interest in the microeconomics of Bangladesh. They are only concerned about the gender of a new dean they are going to recruit. They all like my ideas, presentation, and leadership style but I am unacceptable as a candidate because my anatomy is politically incorrect.

In a course on human diversity and oppression, I usually set the tone of my lectures by explaining the nature of oppressive forces that breed injustice and inequality. India's caste system, I contend, is a primordial model of structured inequality. "We have no caste system in America. Why should we be concerned about caste?" one of the Xers asked. "The United States has the widest equality gap in the industrial world," I replied. I usually lose my audience when I go deeper into the dynamics of basic issues.

Profession X has a chameleon character. As a parasite, this creature has thrived on a unilateral relationship amongst its cognate disciplines. The academic parasitism of social work has cost this discipline its own identity. Paradigms of research, human behavior, social policy, and practice have generated a chaotic confluence of interdisciplinarity that lacks both substance and validity.

Social work is a microcosm of the ethos of culture. One could say, "It's culture, stupid!" A society is both a construct and victim of its own myths. When culture goes sour, one must ask: Is the ethos of today compatible with our ethical and scientific standards? A society that accepts inequality as an imperative of its civilian culture breeds contrapuntal ethics of behavior which stymies progress and thwarts coherent structures of knowledge. As a result of this de-developmental process, a hiatus between problems and policies, individuals and institutions, and art and science permeates both society and culture. This may be called a state of delusional self-absorption. Social work's problems embody this crisis of confidence. Social workers consciously and unconsciously serve as self-fulfilling prophets of a feckless religion—a cult without any color and cause.

NEITHER CLIENTS, NOR PRACTITIONERS

I have taught social work practitioners for about thirty-three years—one third of a century—but I never fully understood the logic and ethic of the client-practitioner paradigm. The obvious reference is to a medical/legal setting where clients seek professional help. In social work's context this is an inappropriate and incorrect role-configuration. Neither we are practitioners, nor are they clients. Social workers and their "clients" constitute a whole that is remarkably different from a medical/legal situation. A surgeon is clinically in control of his/her patient's pathological condition. The procedures that are undertaken for diagnosis and cure are empirically tested and scientifically valid. An attorney's intervention, similarly, is a legal pursuit to redress a "client's" particular claim or grievance. In social practice, human variables and conditions are usually immeasurable and technically unverifiable. The human plasticity of a social situation is qualitatively different than it's medical and legal counterparts. To compare these "apples and oranges" is to confuse the nature of social phenomenon. The politics of social practice has used scientific knowledge to create a smoke screen in front of the causation of social problems, thereby continuing the myth of social illnesses. The accepted notions of etiological causation and therapeutic intervention have confounded areas of problems in manners that are neither humane nor rational. The invincibility of persistent social miseries is a consequence of this misguided scientism.

Albert Camus's relatively unknown *Neither Victims nor Executioners* (1986) raises some pertinent questions about the ethics of our conduct. Camus points the way toward a new ethic of responsibility in coping with the twin threats of contemporary warfare and our own moral culpability in political violence. Can we truly imagine another person's fatal destruction and our own responsibility for it? Can we see ourselves as oppressors and its potential victims at the same time?

It is a freak of the times. We make love by telephone, we work not on matter but on machines, and we kill and are killed by proxy. We gain in cleanliness, but lose in understanding. . . . Here indeed we are Utopian—and contradictory. For we do live, it is true, in a world where murder is legitimate, and we ought to change it if we do not like it. But it appears we cannot change it without risking murder. . . . This much seems clear: Utopia is whatever is in contradiction with reality. [Absolute Utopia is an impossibility.] But a much sounder Utopia is that which insists that murder be no longer legitimized. . . . Relative Utopia is the only realistic choice; it is our last frail hope of saving our skin. (Camus, 1986: 31–41)

Our Brave New World is a reality in living contradictions. We cannot resign from humanity because of ubiguity of problems.

Most of our social problems persist due to moral dilemmas rather than the lack of resources. We invent scapegoats for our collective failures and take comfort in the problem-solving processes that prolong and perpetuate human suffering. The moral equivalents of warfare and violence in social practice are social illfare and injustice that keep the cycle of dehumanizing forces perpetually active. New policies and programs without fundamentally addressing the basic issues create new problems. Menacing cycles of poverty and violence sustain a cancerous culture of social pathologies which scientists blame on the victims of oppression. Contemporary social theory lacks the courage and conviction of calling a spade by its true name. From the "looking glasses" to the "broken windows" we seek refuse in alibis and euphemisms. We dare not speak the truth. We are quiet mercenaries in a trade of tears. We are both accomplice and pimps in a cycle of vice that encompass our whole professional existence.

R. D. Laing once said, "We are all murderers and prostitutes" (Laing, 1967:12). Camus's plea for a shared ethical response is what we lack in professional practice today. All professions, social work included, are guilty of this awful dissonance. A professionally irresponsible culture is encouraging the growth of a narcissistic pattern that has little to do with problem-solution. For lack of a better word, careerism has replaced the ethos of an explorer's quest. Institutional climate and organizational culture breed behaviors that are self-promotive rather than service-oriented. The neolibertarian thrust has uncritically legitimized *laissez-faire* values in the name of efficiency. The efficacy slogans euphemistically promote questionable alliances between marketplace practices and statist policies. The outcome of this postliberal moral debauchery is exemplified in the crises of health care, social welfare, and social justice. While the scourges of poverty, racism, crime, violence, drug, and substance abuse continue to plague the oppressed, intellectuals and scientists continue to manufacture recycled theories and ideas that maintain the mythology of status quo. They speak of a "paradigm shift" without understanding the ramifications of it.

Social scientists' moral culpability underscores an unrecognized state of collective malpractice to which we all may plead guilty in different variations. But for our arrogance and ignorance, this realization may not be as difficult as it may seem. Professional obsessions, egoistic career paths on the one hand and massive neglect of fundamental issues on the other, set up individuals and institutions in a mutually exploitative design in which the "clients" always remain in a no-win situation. In a culture where material success is the ultimate test of one's credibility, means become ends and ends merely play the second fiddle to individualized ambitions. From the White House to the X-School of Social Work, this crisis plagues the whole realm of policy-research-practice paradigm.

IN SEARCH OF A RELATIVE UTOPIA: THE NEW FAUSTIAN IDEOLOGY

In the scheme of things, human affairs are perennially mystified by a sense of primordial ignorance. The roots of evil and the nature of our societal relationships continually puzzle our consciousness. At no other time in human annals we have communicated so much so fast, yet we fail to communicate our deepest feelings to our closet people. This communicative failure is the grand casualty of our civilization. Can we deconstruct the dialogue? Whatever happened to the power of discourse, humans ought to remain humans. I will attempt to portray the banality and innocence of human reality by reconstructing two relatively recent incidents. This will help us understand the nature of our challenges that face humankind.

David Gelernter, a professor of computer science at Yale, was nearly killed when he opened a package that had been mailed to him by a Montana hermit named Theodore Kaczynski. In his thoughtful book *Drawing Life*, the anguished professor writes:

When I looked down at my right hand I saw the bones sticking out in all directions and the skin crumpled like paper. . . . An especially good man represents to a wicked one the ultimate danger—the conscience and justice he hates and can never silence. (Conscience is a Jewish invention, Hitler said; it wouldn't surprise me if the bomber felt the same.) (Gelernter, 1997: 84)

The intellectual world and the Bronx zoo each have two entrances; people who enter the woodsy birdhouse way see the zoo very differently from ones who come in near the Asia department at the far end, with its lotus leaves and camel rides. But it's all one zoo. And art minds are capable of mastering the same intellectual territory as science minds, they merely approach it differently—speaking as an art mind in a scientific trade. (Gelernter, 1997: 86)

A female ape named Binti Jua ("daughter of sunshine") was sitting in her enclosure at Chicago's Brookfield Zoo when a three-year old child fell eighteen feet close to Binti. She gathered the boy gently in her arms and took him to the door where most of his kind usually gathered. "Binti has made clear, she won't do interviews. . . . Fame and oodles of fan mail have not changed her. For example, Binti shared a twenty-five-pound gift of basket bananas with all the zoo's inhabitants," wrote James L. Graff (1996: 70). This "gorilla of America's dream" (Graff, 1996: 70) has lessons for the civilized world. Also, this demonstrated empirical study offers poignant clues to the causes of human tragedy.

A brilliant cartoonist portrays this reality under a study captioned, "The Evolution of Child Care." Scene 1: Welfare Reform Democrat, Washington, D.C.; a toddler is nearly kicked to death by a cruel politician-bureaucrat kind of fat cat. Scene 2: Welfare Reform Republican, Washington, D.C.; another insensitive, apparently rapacious, politician-bureaucrat is kicking this child, who is now lying dead. Scene 3: Gorilla, Brookfield, Ill., Zoo; the baby is finally rescued by an ape who motherly clings it to her bosom (*The Advocate*, 1996: 6B).

If there is an iota of elemental truth in these two incidents, one must revisit the classic issue: What is the genesis of human venality and kindness? And, when exactly did we become evil? Was it during the evolution from ape to Homo sapiens or in the process of social transformation? Or, we are born evil. Perhaps Rousseauean "primitive innocence" turned evil after the emergence of private property is the basis of civil society. The roots of oppression lie somewhere in the twilight of ontogenesis-phylogenesis debates (Mohan, 1993: 19–34).

"From the crooked wood of which man is made, nothing quite straight can be built," said Kant (Becker, 1975: 152). The repugnant heritage, which Sigmund Freud alluded to in his instinctual theory, may seem too pessimistic but the history of humankind offers no optimistic alternatives. Inequality and oppression have been the sources of all societal scourges. Religion and state have perpetuated these inequalities and human destiny seems sealed in a paradoxical cycle of self-perpetuating evil. Reflecting on this new Faustian game, Ernest Becker observes:

Christianity, too, perpetuated this economic inequality and slavishness of the would-be free, democratic citizen; *and there never has been, historically, any fundamental change in the massive structure of domination and exploitation represented by the state after the decline of primitive society.* . . . Not that the promise of the ancient world and of Christianity failed completely. . . . It took the form of a scientific individualism that burst out of the Renaissance and the Reformation. It represented a new power candidate for replacing all the previous ideologies of immortality, but now a new Faustian pursuit of immortality through one's own acts, his own works, his own discovery of truth. This was a kind of secular-humanist immortality based on gifts of the individual. (Becker, 1975: 71; emphasis in original)

The twentieth century, historians warn, is "the darkest" phase of humankind's development (Stern, 1989). The Faustian individual's one-dimensionality is the ultimate failure of all ideologies that flowered in the post-Enlightenment era. Social work mirrors the hope and despair of this failed utopia without the consciousness of a historian. Social work historians simply wallow in the comfort of a pretentious ideology that failed its own people. One can understand this massive

ineffectiveness in a wider social context, as Becker succinctly summarizes below, but the moral naivete and intellectual bankruptcy of
Unfaithful Angels (Specht and Courtney, 1994) is both indefensible
and pathetic.

History and its incredible tragedy and drivenness then become a record of
understandable folly. It is the career of a frightened animal who must lie in
order to live—or, better, in order to live the distinctive style that his nature
fits him for. The thing that feeds the great destructiveness of history is that
men give their entire allegiance to their own group; and each group is a
codified hero system. Which is another way of saying that societies are stan-
dardized systems of death denial; they give structure to the formulas for
heroic transcendence. History can then be looked at as a succession of immortality ideologies or as a mixture at any time of several of these ideologies.
(Becker, 1975: 153–154)

The crisis of social work emanates from its cultural womb. The modern social work culture, politically Eurocentric, is hopelessly narcissistic. Even the so-called internationalists in this field deify a hero
system with the anxieties of a frightened animal. The imperial-
material power that American affluence affords to these self-
proclaimed pundits of a new Faustian ideology simply perpetuates the
old follies of a bygone era.

The nineteenth century thinkers thought of a unitary approach to
study the human condition in relation to its holistic origins. The
realization of the philosophy of this existential heritage reached back
to the Enlightenment. However, "it fell to the twentieth century to
reap all the bitter fruits of the dispersal of a unitary conception of
experience: science in the service of destruction; mankind converted
into mindless consumer masses, rocked this way and that by sensa-
tional news items and by strong demagogues" (Becker, 1968: 307–
308).

Social work's origins lie in the forces of reconstruction that underscored the significance of the wholeness of experience and creation
of a meaningful social reality that symbolized a less unhappy, better
society. As a professional discipline, however, it grew up with innate
fissures and contradictions relative to the conception of the human
condition. Our concerns, responses, and strategies continue to reflect
these unresolved conflicts.

Epistemologically and organizationally, social work deals with issues with a pervasive dualism which is usually self-defeating. The ramifications of this unresolved dualism are reflected in the continuing conflicts of our epistemological polemics. We resort to medical-institutional approaches unmindful of the eco-environmental influences that impact human behavior. Also, we blame society for all our learned and innate deficits. A blaming-game thus obscures the genesis of our problems. The Garden of Eden is fraught with the serpents of desires and fascination for apples. If humankind is left locked in this tragic situation, there is no hope for survival. The Hobbesians may have already won. However, Binti Jua can instruct us all if we give up our expert pretensions.

In a fascinating book, *Ishmael*, a gorilla instructs his pupil, a civilized human being, about the wretchedness of the latter's civilization (Quinn, 1993). He offers a prescription:

Then here is a program. The story of Genesis must be reversed. First, Cain must stop murdering Abel. This is essential if you're to survive. The Leavers are the endangered species most critical to the world—not because they're humans but because they alone can show the destroyers of the world that there is no *one right way* to live. And then, of course, you must spit out the fruit of that forbidden tree. You must absolutely and forever relinquish the idea that you know who should live and who should die on this planet. (Quinn, 1993: 248)

Anthropocentrism has had a corrupting influence on the development of human psyche. One of the fundamental issues in the history of science has been consciousness construction leading to human freedom. Human emancipation, however, is a continuous saga. The ontology of science, from a humanistic point of view, is a liboratory process. Since neither medicine nor law is a perfect science, one can argue that qualitative (art and values) aspect is the legitimizing qualification of a scientific practice. Social work, therefore, has a scientific rationale without being a science.

Empirical objectivity is modernity's greatest myth. Did Carl Sagan actually see a black hole? Deification of evidence has mystified scientific objectivity as a new cult. The objectivity cult, in turn, has created its own believers. A higher form of orthodoxy, unless demystification assumes a higher priority, will thwart the development of progressive consciousness.

Social workers are people who have studied and learnt the art and science of caring. This professional endeavor involves a litany of roles, goals, and strategies as conceptualized by the skilled pioneers in the field. The specialty of caring for others in distress is as old as human nature. Perhaps civilization would not develop if all mortals were inherently cannibalistic. The innate need to survive and perpetuate intensified latent pugnacity but it also enhanced the learned, or innate, benevolence which is the fount of all altruism.

Altruism, unlike technology, is categorically a benevolent manifestation of human creativity. "Technology happens," Andrew Grove, *Time*'s "Man of the Year," clips. "It's not good, it's not bad. Is steel good or bad?" (Isaacson, 1997–1998: 50). Modernity's exclusive claim over the entire scientific domain is at best exaggerated. One can argue that civilizational advancements have benumbed the inherent benevolence and created a culture in which people are less humane to each other. The rise of individualism and materialism at the expense of a communal support system is proof of modernity's inadvertent callousness about basic unfulfilled human needs. The manufacturers and inventors of steel and microchips did not think critically and socially; their motives were evidently quite self-serving. Bill Gates and Ted Turner's charitable funds are not going to solve world poverty. Unless we re-invent science, human misery will continue to be our challenge. Social work, therefore, seeks to benefit from science in its service to humanity without becoming a tool of its oppression. This may well be the defining distinction between social work and general altruism commonly practiced by others.

"Kids who care" demonstrate that common sense, commitment, and care are innate impulses of a concerned people and their achievements exemplify model outcomes for academically trained social workers (Agrest, 1997: 132–134). Susan Agrest has spotlighted certain icons of benign human ingenuity whose articulate vision and skilled conduct dwarfs the "outcomes" of professional practice:

Calendar Girl: Annia Burns at age fifteen was troubled by inequity and one day found herself turning to the section of human services in the telephone book. She began to dial. Her call to the Embry Rucker Community Shelter, a facility that houses homeless children in nearby Reston, would better not only the lives of hundreds of children but Annia's life as well.

Role Reversal: Aaron Soto, thirteen, traded places with his former East Picacho Elementary School teachers . . . [and] ran through a series of sophisticated videoconferencing demonstrations.

Jessica's Feat: Jessica Burris, fourteen, lives life to the hilt every day. . . . Jessica currently has twenty kids her age volunteering for Sock It to Me. Now they also collect shoes, clothing, toiletries, and money for medication to benefit thousands of people.

On the Fast Track: Cecelia-Nan Ding, seventeen, senior at the Boston Latin School, finds the number of calls made to Boston's shelters disturbing. . . . Despite the rhetoric condemning abuse, says Nan, statistics like these prove that domestic violence is "institutionalized" in our society. . . . To help remedy the problem, Nan, this past June, started a company called FAST (Friends and Shelter for Teens). . . . Nan has twenty-five teen volunteers working with her, most of them recruited from her school.

Team for Life: In Coach Ryan Brimer's eyes, everyone is a winner. . . . These days, now twenty, Ryan leads his players, some of whom are disabled, in a warm-up, encouraging them to have fun in a Special Olympics program called Unified Sports.

Taking ACTION: Sipfou Saechao, seventeen, Contra Coasta County, California, has broken down racial barriers and, in this wretched environment, against all these obstacles, she has not only flourished but become a leader.

Marked by MAGIC: A high school club creates an urban oasis. Adam Hornstine, sixteen, in Camden, New Jersey, founded a high school club named MAGIC (Moorsetown Alliance for Goodwill and Interest in Community).

On the Board: Cory Kadamani, seventeen, is one of the creators of the fledgling South Bronx Community Justice Center in New York City; he serves as both volunteer and employee at the center, a project of a well-regarded community organization called Youth Force. . . . Cory is looking out of lots of windows these days. . . . At John Jay High School in affluent Westchester County recently Cory introduced "Busting Stereotypes," a series of skits that show how one can make false assumptions about people. A homeless kid from the South Bronx, Cory himself is as powerful a symbol of misplaced assumptions as anyone is likely to find. (Agrest, 1997: 132–134)

Five teens "who are changing the world," were recently winners of *react* magazine's Take Action Award. "For improving their school, community, nation or the world, each got a $20,000 scholarship from the New World Foundation plus $25,000 for needy children in their community," reports Jane Ciabattari (1997: 19). They are:

Aaron Gordon, fifteen, of Miami. He crusaded to make school bus safety a national priority and co-authored a federal bill requiring new buses to have safety belts. He is also working to require other safety features.

Anisa Kintz, fourteen, of Conway, South Carolina. At eight she founded
  Calling All Colors, a racial-unity conference for grades three to eight.
  Now an annual event, it has spread across the United States and to Canada
  and New Zealand.

Melissa Poe, seventeen, of Nashville. She founded Kids for Clean Environment, now with 300,000 members worldwide.

Rosina Roibal, seventeen, of Albuquerque, New Mexico. An environmen-
  talist, she is working to stop the building of two roads through Petroglyph
  National Monument.

Michael Tan, eighteen, of Irvine, California. Regional President of the California Association of Student Councils, he helps organize programs that
  teach students how to make things happen. He also is a member of his
  school board. (Ciabattari, 1997: 19)

These exemplars of civil responsibility and fundamental altruism represent the hope and despair of a civilization that has lost its hold on
its founding values. Anu Sharma, my daughter, prefers to treat children in clinical medical practice despite daunting challenges in a
Bronx hospital. "Children are hapless victims of irresponsible par-
enthood," she expertly contends with the authority of a qualified pe-
diatrician (Sharma, 1997). Not unlike Anu's inadvertent clients, victims of injustice and oppression cry for help. The case studies of
"Kids who care" (Agrest, 1997; Ciabattari, 1997) exemplify the need
for human concern as well as the art of institutionalizing modalities
and practices that sustain human dignity. Are there any unique, specialized features of such endeavors that characterize individual and
group efforts as a specialized professional behavior? The twentieth
century social workers contend that their roles and goals have acquired a professional status. From Flexner (1915) to David Austin
(1997), intellectuals in the field have argued for and against social
work's professional attributes. Yet, even the most advanced social
work practice has seldom produced a model that would nearly match
the outcomes of the "Kids who care" (Agrest, 1997). Then, why social
work?
  A study of the behavior, environment, and values of these young
idealist-activist boys and girls is suggestive of numerous lessons that
social work students, practitioners, educators, and researchers ought
to learn. Three main conclusions may be driven from the analysis of
these case studies which have ramifications on our entire professional
culture. First, social work as a career is not going to solve any social

problems. It may, if thoughtfully designed and delivered, help facilitate some understanding of issues at best. Second, the knowledge, skills, and values that social workers espouse are no exclusive domains of our schools, agencies, and departments. A genuine interest in community affairs and a resolute will to help change the human condition is far more an effective agent of change than a D.S.W. or a Ph.D. degree in social work. Third, social work's specialized competencies, fields, and methods constitute a self-serving paladin of professional politics that serves various interest groups without directly and positively impacting the lives of any oppressed groups. This skepticism validates the legitimacy crisis of social work as a profession. It's not merely effectiveness; it's basic authenticity and legitimacy that are at issue.

The New World order is creating new opportunities and challenges. To seize the ethos of the moment involves acceptance of new social-human realities, which in turn implies our commitment—beyond accreditation standards—to certain basic premises and postulates that should constitute the *zeitgeist*. Specifically, it means three objectives:

1. A sense of civil responsibility for caring and sharing;
2. A commitment to root out the forces of oppression; and
3. A realization that any change in the existing human condition is impossible until social justice is accepted and pursued as a mega project of universal well-being.

"A sense of responsibility for the rest of the world," in Vaclav Havel's words means, "a deep respect for everything that in today's multipolar and multicultural world constitutes 'otherness,' a respect acquired from understanding the positive values in other cultures" (Havel, 1998: 24).

At the same time it means the courage to step away from power mongering and, in a non-violent way, to defend truth and justice wherever they are violated, regardless of whether this could put profit at risk. It means trying to be on the side of good, without being motivated by considerations of power or economic interests, thus exposing their hypocrisy. It means promoting tolerance and understanding among nations and religions, enhancing all forms of international cooperation and regional integration aimed at the general good. It means creating the space for a wise attitude toward Nature and the Earth, an attitude that sees human beings as an integral part of Nature, not as its masters, proprietors, or wanton exploiters. (Havel, 1998: 24)

The above quote is cited from President Havel's address in Washington on October 3, 1997, after receiving the Fulbright Prize. The relevance of his words cannot be gainsaid in a profession which enchants the mantras of diversity, equality, and international understanding without addressing social justice against all forms of human-social oppression. The "sociology of social work," as I know it, as I feel it, and as I see it revolves around a career path that entails self-promotion without "a sense of responsibility for the rest of the world" (Havel, 1998: 24).

I agree with Havel's observation that "contemporary America is an almost symbolic concentration of all the best and worst of our civilization" (Havel, 1998: 24; Mohan, 1985a). Since social work is shaped and practiced as a microcosm of the American culture, one could say the same thing about the profession as a whole. I have seen savants, sages, and scholars in this profession; I have also come across hypocrites and bigots whose professional conduct borders on unabashed thievery without any sense of remorse. The challenge is to eschew the mundane benefits of power and realize the essence of human dignity in relation to others in a concrete and human fashion without a voracious self-serving stance and style.

The second and third objectives that I have formulated above relate to the very soul of our profession. The theme of oppression has lately become the "sexiest" new subject. I consider it to be a welcome sign but it cannot be called progressive until the root causes of oppression are scientifically analyzed, studied, and ameliorated. The profession pays lip service to its mandated goals. As soon as a site visit for the reaccredidation is over, we tend to regress with a sense of complacence, comfort, and relief. An impressive window dressing is usually a cover to hide ugly realities. A total commitment to social justice is not yet in the professional cards. Themes about social and economic justice are being introduced in certain courses. At least two prestigious schools have organized specialization in social and economic justice but the general framework of curricula designs and their delivery remain heavily skewed in favor of careerist, profit-making, self-serving modalities which permeate the entire culture of the profession and society as a whole. To analyze social justice and talk about it in a social policy course or in a particular specialization is one thing; to organize the whole curriculum around this premise and unify it with research, human behavior, practice, and all forms of practica is another. It is my contention that the interface between the human condition and social justice ought to be the single most important unifying basis of social work education, practice, and research. The unification of knowledge is not only a scientific mandate; it also is a humanistic imperative. If social work fails to acknowledge and implement this imperative as a mandate, future generations of social workers will continue to strive for their identity and mission. I seriously doubt if we have been able to invent our future; our continued dependence on others is a sign of our self-deserved devolution.

In sum, social work masquerades as a euphemism in a culture that promotes acquisitive-hedonistic pursuits under the cover of altruism lacking both authenticity as well as legitimacy. Its professional domain is a self-proclaimed territory that remains under constant attacks by rival, often lesser, occupations that demand a piece of pie in the name of freedom and service. As an academic specialty, it remains a second class citizen in the community of established disciplines without any rigorous effort to assert its identity. Its "otherness" thus emanates from a cultural neurosis that sustains inherent contradictions. Liberatory constentation unconfounded by ideological fissures and epistemic resistance is bound to generate a fuller view of social reality denied so far by an incomplete profession. "Discovery of a truth by oneself without suggestion or outside help is creation," wrote Antonio Gramsci, "even though the truth is an old one" (Gramsci, [1957] 1992: 132). Emphasizing the importance of the unitary principle in the transformation of all organs of culture, especially professional specialties, Gramsci diagnosed the cause of modern crisis in these words:

Moreover, today's widespread educational crisis can be precisely linked to the fact that this process of differentiation and specialization has taken place chaotically, without clear and precise principles, without a well thought out and consciously fixed plan. The crisis in educational programmes and organization, that is, of the general direction of a policy for developing modern intellectual cadres, is to a large extent an aspect and complication of a more comprehensive and general organic crisis. (Gramsci, 1957: 126)

2

Self, Society, and Science: On Transforming Social Reality

Human nature constitutes a treaty in itself, and human beings are far more effectively united by kindness than by contracts, by feelings than by words.

—Thomas Moore (1965: 109)

Construction of social reality is a dialectical outcome of epistemic and social pressures. Sociology of scientific knowledge, therefore, situates science in an ontological context. This chapter posits social reality, social theory, and social transformation in a unifying mode. By implication social reality becomes the focal point of scientific analysis and liberatory praxis; social reality, and its reconstruction, precede transformational processes. An argument is offered against the science and method that seek validation without aesthetico-axiological basis.

My social reality reflects the hope and despair of a ligustrum scented community that blissfully wallows in the swamps of unreason. The writer's challenge "is to reveal, demonstrate, demystify, and dissolve myths and fetishes in a critical acid bath," says Jean Paul Sartre ([1974] 1983: 299). "Don't forget that a man carries the whole epoch with him, just like a wave carries the whole sea. . . . The need to write is fundamentally a quest for purification" (Sartre, [1974] 1983: 32).

"A science which hesitates to forget its founders is lost" (Whitehead,

1961: 25; emphasis added). The Whiteheadian aphorism has come to haunt the flat-earthers of the utopian sciences. "A clash of doctrines is not a disaster—it is an opportunity," wrote Alfred North White-head (1961: 175). The post–Cold War reality posits science and progress in a critical context and the essence of education calls for renewed examination. Unless a melting pot of re-examinations and refutations becomes a credible reality, scientific process as a whole remains a fragmented exercise unrelated to the goal of the Enlightenment. Certain fallacies of progress mark the end of knowledge as a liberatory process and social sciences are no exception to this postmodern barbarity. The great divide of social theory—between structure (society) and action (agency)—has balkanized knowledge to the extent that the interdisciplinary Holy Grail—the systems theory—appears to be the end of science itself.

PREMISES AND POSTULATES

Human, social, and scientific advancements have a common purpose: enlightenment and social well-being. The universal indicators of progress are related to but not dependent on mere economic, cognitive, and technological success. The social systems—their ideology and organization—offer pertinent contexts to assessing the extent and quality of societal development. Yet social-scientific "paradigms" (Kuhn, [1962] 1996) lack a unifying rationale to study global issues. A psychologist has lately argued that "dysrationalia"—the inability to function rationally in spite of cognitive intelligence—is a horrendous social problem (Stanovich, 1994). Many contrapuntal signs are visible on the national and international horizons that testify to the existence of "dysrationalia" in the realm of social practice. A new tribalism permeates disciplines, specialties, services as well as communities of peoples. This loss of Rousseauean "primitive innocence" is a global tragedy that represents the monumental failure of scientific knowledge. If equality and justice are the main universal values, clues to the global malaise may be found in the bedrock of critical social theory with certain value judgements.[1] Three premises underline this analysis:

• Selfhood as an extension of human autonomy and fulfillment;

• Society as a reality of abstraction conducive to human existence; and,

• "Scientificity" (Foucault, [1972] 1993: 184) as a liberatory process, compatible with the goal of the Enlightenment.

Science as a value-free endeavor is an objective myth. Truth, as Sartre tells us, "is an intersubjective matter" (Sartre, 1992: xiv). In other words, inter-individuality occupies a central position at the intersection of history and existence. We will examine these premises and our postulated constructs in light of relevant developments in social theory that relate to social practice. This framework helps unravel the complexity and interrelatedness of various units of analysis toward a unifying theory of social transformation (Figure 2.1). This analysis is shown in the context of social theory:

Units of Analysis	*Social Theory: Main Theoretical Traditions*
Self	Psychoanalysis
Society	Theories of Social Action, Structure, and Conflict
Science and Knowledge	Scientism, Positivism, and Critical Social Theory

Social reality, in the realm of science, remains a contentious subject. Post-empiricists (Feyerabend [1975] 1988; Rorty, 1979) assert that social reality is a construct of knowledge producers rather than an outcome of scientific rationality. "In the dialectic between nature and the socially constructed world," Peter Berger and Thomas Luckmann argued, "the human organism itself is transformed" (Berger and Luckmann, 1966: 183). The quality of being human is what we come to know as social reality. In practice, by and large, social scientists follow a functional view of the human condition and uncritically resort to pragmatic methods. A unified view of self, society, and science is sadly lost in the fog of postmodern ideological conflict. Pretentious quarrels with science have only generated a "higher superstition" (Gross and Levitt, 1994). This chapter is an argument toward a unifying theory of social transformation (Figure 2.1).

Critically, social theory and "scientificity" (Foucault, 1972: 184) interface the intertwined domains of social reality and human experience. "Ideology is not exclusive of scientificity," says Michel Foucault (1972: 186). We employ social theory "to explain and understand experience on the basis of other experiences and general ideas about the world" (Craib, 1985: 7–8). Much of modern social theory, Ian Craib contends, centers around social action, symbolic interactionism, conflict, and structuralism (Craib, 1985). Randall Collins

Figure 2.1
Social Reality in the Realm of Science

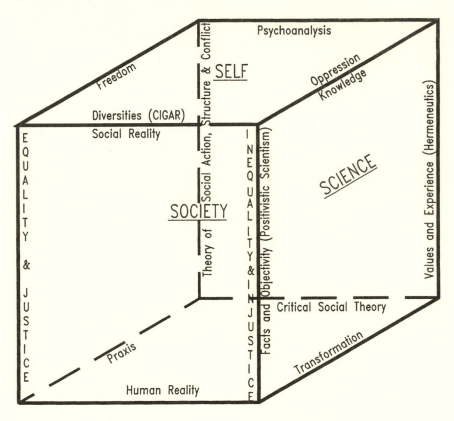

Toward a Unifying Theory of Social Transformation

has analyzed four major sociological traditions to demonstrate the progress of knowledge of the social world. These traditions include: the conflict, the rational/utilitarian, the Durkheimian, and the microinteractionalist (Collins 1994; 1994a). Of particular interest to us is *social theory as science* that helps "unification of the science of [people]" (Becker, 1968). A synthesized view of these approaches is employed here toward a new formulation: social reality as the focal object of social transformation. This implies a holographic—three dimensionally critical—view of the human-social reality in professional theory and discursive practice (Figure 2.1).

Ideology, existing social values and structures, and the level of scientific knowledge define the content and character of analysis of a given subject in a particular spatio-temporal context. Immanuel Kant revolutionized the world of knowledge by unifying the empirical and rational conceptions of reality (Kant, 1958). Neo-Kantian and post-structuralist contributions have further expanded our cognitive-philosophical horizons. A discussion on racism and sexism, for example, in the American culture of the nineties is qualitatively different than those occurred before the sixties. Similarly, the individual-and-society relationship issues are different in the post-communist era at the "end of history" (Fukuyama, 1989). Social theory, as an interpretation of science, history, and praxis, incessantly questions the conjectures and formulations impacting social reality. Is the "end of history" real or surreal? Is the loss of a democratic party in a particular country the end of democratic process? If there is any thing universal about social justice and equality, then, obsolescence of egalitarian values seems to be a prejudgment. Presumption, which precedes prejudgment, is therefore illogical and irrational. The nauseous-oppressive aspects of human reality—inequality and injustice—are inherently involved in the dialectics of human freedom (Mohan, 1987; 1988; 1993; 1996).

SELF, SOCIETY, AND SCIENCE

Flight from the reality of selfhood, as Kierkegaard said, characterizes the modern human situation (Kierkegaard, [1849] 1941). Kierkegaard's despair unto death underscored the sin at the bottom—deep in the human psyche. Freudian and Marxian views, looking at the individual from outside, postulated deterministic theories that find causes of neurosis external to self. In the post-Freudo-Marxian era, one should be able to synthesize the causes of malady that bedevils civilizational growth. The Americanization of psychoanalysis, Norman Birnbaum contends, "emptied Freud's own work of historical and philosophical meaning" (Birnbaum, 1988: 78). Emancipation, however, continues to be a common theme in the neo-Freudo-Marxian critiques. While Erich Fromm revived Marxist humanism (Fromm, 1941), and Norman Brown dismissed social conflict as an epiphenomenon in the play of fundamental psychic forces (Brown

1959), Herbert Marcuse developed the notions of "surplus repression" and "repressive desublimation" enabling us to think of a situation in which emancipation would be made possible by the historical development of psyche (Marcuse, 1955; 1964; Birnbaum, 1988: 78–79, 207). Birnbaum specifies three relevant themes that have developed in America: (1) narcissism (Kohut, 1971; Lasch, 1978); (2) the theory of separation; and (3) the process of internalization (Birnbaum, 1988: 79–83). Secularization of social theory has impacted the delivery of social sciences but educational processes remain hollow without critical theoretical content. Social work practitioners' disdain for social theory is an outcome of this flawed development.

Even though Freud exposed the glittering darkness of the Victorian values, the psychoanalytic movement—if critiqued from the humanist variables of race, gender, and class—has neglected diversity issues in general. A politically correct version has not yet achieved momentum despite the gains of the feminist movement. As we emphasize human diversity, issues of race, gender, and class are gaining, albeit slowly, recognition as dimensions of a new unfreedom (Mohan, 1993; 1996). Feminist ethics of alternative culture and life styles also demythologize certain Freudian myths about self, society, and science. *Ally McBeal* notwithstanding (Bellafante, 1998: 54–62), Lisa Jones' *Bulletproof Diva* (1994) and Barbara Ehrenreich's *Hearts of Men* (1983) are formidable critiques of the American society. Yet, social reality as a secular universe of human autonomy, remains an incomplete project.

Liberation of society, Marcuse contends, is possible through psychoanalytical understanding (Marcuse, 1970). A progressive synthesis of Freudian-Marxian contributions has been a monumental gift of the Frankfurt School of Social Relations. It was no accident that Columbia University in New York and not Harvard in Cambridge offered the Frankfurt Institute the hospitality in the United States (Birnbaum, 1988: 4). Jurgen Habermas presented psychoanalysis as "the only tangible example of a science incorporating methodical self-reflection" (Habermas, 1972: 214), and thus as a model for the general epistemology of a critical social theory guided by the emancipatory interest in human autonomy (Keat, 1981: 94). Critical theorists' self-reflective unification of historical-hermeneutic process—involving "theory" and "practice"—seems to validate a rationale for the praxis of transformation.

Views of science, according to Jerome R. Ravetz, vary as "the pursuit of truth," "technocratic conception," "humanist critique," and "dirty work" (Ravetz, 1971: 12–30). Today's science is fraught with numerous social and ethical problems. "Industrialization of science," Ravetz contends, implies "the domination of capital-intensive research, and its social consequences in the concentration of power in a small section of the community" (Ravetz, 1971: 30). The loss of innocence of science has deeper ramifications for both the individual and the society than the industrialization of production and adulteration of products of research implies. The abuses of the "shoddy science" and the rise of a pretentious, self-serving leadership in academia represent the evils of a society that has lost its moral compass and, sadly, the will to reinvent it. Ravetz's conclusion is instructive to social scientists:

Thus in spite of its great achievements, and indeed because of some of them, the world of natural science faces serious problems of an entire new order. . . . Indeed, the social sciences themselves, and sophisticated technology as well, have analogous problems. The solutions, if there be any, cannot be imposed from outside by the fiat of politicians or administrators; scientific inquiry is too complex and delicate to be treated like the production of commodities. . . . Whether the present conditions are propitious for the emergence of such a leadership will be known only by those who look back from the future. (Ravetz: 1971: 68)

SOCIAL REALITY AND THE CORRUPTION OF SCIENCE: THE "END OF SYSTEMS"?

If " 'having,' 'doing,' and 'being' are the cardinal categories of human reality," as Sartre wrote (Sartre, [1953] 1966: 527), social reality is the awareness of the human situation: experience, events, arrangements, and one's consciousness of this complex milieu. In other words, the cardinal ingredients of social reality involve an individual's worldview, a consciousness of his/her existential situation. This awareness of reality is both subjective and objective at the same time. To bifurcate the two is to commit violence against rationality and humanity. Also, as Sartre puts it, "judgement is an interdividual phenomenon" (Sartre, 1992: xiv). Social indicators quantify the quality of life issues without alluding to the essence of human reality. One may be rich and famous yet murderously dangerous and alienated.[2] Quantitism is, therefore, a false paradigm of human fulfillment. The pain of hunger cannot be quantified; the indignation against discrimination cannot be measured; and the terror of a vile authority cannot be check listed. Yet, pain, indignation, and terror constitute the core of this dehumanized experience. Political abuse of bureaucracy and psychiatry often represent ominous manifestations of social control to eliminate the voices of dissent.[3]

In addition to perceptual and cognitive structures, sociological and political elements help organize a sense of social reality. Race, gender, and class, for example, help identify the main determinations of one's social reality. In a diverse society, especially in the democratic world, construction of social reality must be the agenda of all national and international policies of development. This, simultaneously, involves both deconstruction as well as reconstruction of social processes. To avoid the epistemological confusion of the post-modernist jargon, we must espouse "new global development" (Mohan, 1997a) heralded by the age of Enlightenment. The "Enlightenment paradox" (Becker, 1968: 360), which alienated its own mandate, is perhaps the best reason for launching the Enlightenment II. Scientific revolution, Thomas Kuhn says, implies deep and sudden destructive departure from traditional "paradigms" (Kuhn, 1962). Kuhnian historiography seemingly posits "normal" and social sciences in a dichotomous context. Is the end of knowledge in sight?

The ends of "ideology" (Bell, 1960), "history" (Fukuyama, 1989), "philosophy" (Rorty, 1989), "equality" (Kaus, 1992), "sociology" (Birnbaum, 1988: 220) and even "physics" (Lindley, 1993) demystify the myths of a universal paradigm. For more than a century, David Lindley contends scientists have struggled to find the Holy Grail: a unifying theory that would make sense of the entire universe; but a "theory of every thing" has been an illusion. Lindley warns that the compromises necessary to produce a final theory may well undermine the rules of doing good science (Lindley, 1993).

The need for "good science" is mandated in the basic covenants of scientific inquiry and research. Politicization, industrialization, and bureaucratization of knowledge have corrupted scientific processes with the result that the search for truth, human emancipation, and freedom has become secondary objectives. This displacement of scientific goal, if you will, reconstitutes the new "structure of evil" (Becker, 1968).

Scientific disciplines, Stephan Fuchs theorizes, are invisible organizations which "have their own hierarchy of power; they control access to material resources such as lab equipment, jobs, journals, and book publishing" (Fuchs 1992: xv–vi). A "reflexive sociology of science," Fuchs comments, calls for "Hermeneutics as Deprofessionalization" (Fuchs, 1992: 193–214). Fuchs' conclusion may be read with optimism and challenge:

I have argued that hermeneutics and interpretivism have not so much to do with ontology of social worlds but with the ways in which social research is socially organized. . . . [W]e could have something like a "mature science of society" without a hermeneutic problem if the discipline was more closely integrated and fully professionalized. . . . We will engage in hermeneutics and conversation rather than in science and fact production as long as the structure of our profession remains loosely organized. But, we might not want to change that, for the conversational life form is more pleasant than a bureaucratic one. (Fuchs, 1992: 214–215)

The organizational reality of contemporary sciences is neither conversational nor interpretive; it is sadly archaic and opaque. In a social world rampant with racism, xenophobia, and predatory competition on the one hand and corporate avarice, greed, and illfare on the other, one cannot expect the triumph of reflective values and egalitarian outcomes. A new culture of corporate fascism seems to promote a cult of leadership and effectiveness that is both repugnant and anti-intellectual. The university organization zealously maintains a caste system that rewards and recognizes its own Brahmins. Teachers and researchers, especially in non-marketable specialties have become the new "shudras" (untouchables) in this bureaupathic system of inequality. The fundraising hysteria, however pragmatic, has virtually sold out the academic freedom to a new class of donors, administrators, and information machinists whose alliances are not always holy. Massive apathy and demoralization of the intellectual community mark this alienation of the educational process as a whole. Those academics and intellectuals whose specialties benefit the corporate sector maintain a high mobility and profile; others merely survive and languish in an otherwise academically free setting. The cult of efficiency lends arbitrary power in administrative echelons that use the Draconian prowess to execute an agenda of their own interests. The autonomous status of the academic settings almost legitimizes institutional unaccountability which, I contend, is the incubator of academic corruption, mismanagement, uncommitted instruction, and inauthentic, shoddy, and/or spurious research. Furthermore, the politics—not logic—of race, gender, and class has promoted new sectors of privileged groups that demand recognition without merit. This corruption of rationality and humanity is a perversion of scientific values; its outcome is a distorted view of social reality.

REINVENTING SOCIAL PRACTICE: RESPONSES TO NEW NATIONAL AND GLOBAL CHALLENGES

Academic social work is a product of institutional traditions and societal values. The professional status of theory and practice is an outcome of these competing, often conflictive power structures. Social work theory is an oxymoronic formulation. Social work's parasitism thrives on multi-disciplinary exchanges without its own epistemology. Social theory's dynamism underscores an interdisciplinary base for a creative system of social work education, practice, and research (SW-EPR; Mohan, 1988: 63–64) but contemporary social work models, especially in the United States, continue to follow a positivist-functionalist logic.[4] Human reality and social phenomenon—in a "counterintuitive era" (Gibbs, 1994: 30)—are entering into a new analytical marriage where dichotomous interpretations are becoming obsolete. Indeed, a unified model of social work is what the profession needs at the intersection of science and humanity (Mohan, 1993a). A new phenomenological ontology of the post-Cold war existence is in order to capture the essence of a contrapuntal reality.

Globalization of economy, democracy, and science is changing the patterns of relationships, specialties, communications, and institutional designs. Yet, "the best medium of communication remains, not the fiber-optic cable, but the common thread of humanity" (Baird, 1994: 7). There are encouraging signs of secularization and progress; there is unsettling evidence of professional archaism, rational ossification, and ideological regression. The result is a less transparent, more bureaucratic social world that is unwilling to recognize the structure of new evils: obsolete curricular designs; unscientific research models; self-serving leadership; anti-dialogical settings; crassness of careerism, and a nearly cannibalistic pursuit of success. While these are generalized anomalies of academia, individualized disciplines and settings do manifest symptoms of this "syndrome" in varying degree. Also, one's sense of social reality may be a contributing factor.

An unprincipled success may be vulgar pragmatism to "X"; it may yield a badge of honor to "Y." The point is: institutions and agencies are microcosms of a society that puts premium on material success unrelated to one's demonstrated value commitments. Success orientation normally wins at the expense of value orientation. The outcome of this situation is unlikely to be progressive. Alienation and apathy will be reflected in low personnel morale and high occupational stress.[5] Productivity as well as effectiveness are bound to suffer at a terrible cost to the society.

Social work as a discipline is still not a "first class citizen" on most university campuses. Individual "success" stories are exceptions of institutional politics. The "reflexive sociology" (Fuchs, 1992: xvii) of social work, social welfare, and social development calls for a new consciousness which is quite an indelible challenge. The politics of science, ethnicity, and intra-institutional factions have generated new tribalism that systematically alienates certain people on the basis of CIGAR—class, ideology, gender, age, and race (Mohan, 1993: 56). It is ironic that the evilness of this acronym should paralyze the soul of a profession that prides itself on its diversity and egalitarian ethics. A crisis of identity permeates the whole system of social work. The coherence of a unifying theme that must reverberate the entirety of SW-EPR is missing in the methodological polemics of professional practice.[6] William Epstein's findings reveal an alarming state of social work's science and art:

Social services themselves are the dramas of social myth that are scripted by the social sciences. . . . Social work's flat-earthers dominate the field. . . . The scientific eccentricities of social work are indulged by a society that takes comfort in the lap of its fables. Successful social work does not imply helping people solving their problems. To the contrary, it means successfully promoting the symbols of cheap cure at the expense of those people. The severe economic and budgetary pinches on the poor of the last decade or so have not awakened the field's researchers out of their psychotherapeutic reveries. . . . [T]he poor research in social work suggests a cultish betrayal of the spirit of science. . . . In denying science, the field denies benevolence. (Epstein, 1993: 17, 96, 97–99)

Social work's epistemological foundations are based on academic parasitism, unreflective view of social reality, and uncritical self-awareness. The usual outcome is a self-congratulatory report on a pretentious individual and/or institutional leadership that seeks "comfort in the lap of its fables," to paraphrase Epstein (1993: 97). Social work's flat-earthers go beyond domination; they are reinventing a reductionist wheel that is both myopic and unscientific. A cross-sectional review of institutional settings and curriculum designs and offerings in America would reveal a dogged adherence to archaic leadership styles and loosely organized, untested concepts of systems theory without a philosophical understanding of wider implications. It is common experience that social work faculty and students abhor deeper discussions on philosophical-critical issues. Without exaggeration, the social work culture is expediently anti-intellectual. In the third world, India for example, social work is practiced on imported constructs and methods without any relationship to social reality. There is, however, a greater sense of openness and exchange toward the reconstruction of an ill-suited strategy (Mohan, 1993a).

The problem of ineffective social methodologies—faulty strategies, flawed policies, shoddy research, counterproductive practice, unrealistic program design, the theory-practice hiatus, regressive leadership, and inefficiency of measurement and evaluation—emanates from three major sources (1) scientists' and practitioners' sense of social reality; (2) organizational context of research, teaching, and learning; and (3) social climate and its political persuasion that seek reaffirmation from the professional and scientific community. A combination of these forces generates a myriad of conceptualizations, methods, and modalities that usually promote counterproductivity and even dysfunctionality. Crises of the American medical and social welfare systems manifestly epitomize this tragic syndrome.

Social work education, practice, and research (SW-EPR) is a process that does not occur in a social vacuum; politico-cultural determinations dictate its content and character (Mohan, 1988). Social work literature, Epstein laments, "is mind-numbing repetition of graven pieties, a barren landscape of small-sample, biased, uncontrolled quantitism" (Epstein 1994: 134–136). "In the epistemological realm," Frederic Reamer says, "contemporary social workers need to gain a better understanding of the evolution of debate about the role of science in practice" (Reamer, 1993: 198). Our *Unfaithful Angels* (Specht and Courtney, 1994) represent the end of a noble tradition. Our mission calls for reinvention (Mohan, 1995). The national and international social reality is a complex creature of historico-temporal anomalies and ironies. A New World order has created a world disorder, which dwarfs the monstrosities of the American welfare system. From Bosnia to Rwanda and Haiti to Tibet, one hears the echoes of barbarism, death, and chaos. While most American social workers contend with private practice with the victims of sexual, spousal, and substance abuse,[7] realities within national boundaries and beyond call for a radical transformation of the purpose and method of the profession itself. The inability to seize this challenge amounts to the end of social work, as we knew. The awareness, however, calls for a new social work (Mohan, 1996b).

"Science must be protected from ideologies," warns Paul Feyerabend, "and societies, especially democratic societies, must be protected from science" (Feyerabend, 1975: viii). Separation of science and state, Feyerabend argues, is perhaps the most daunting challenge that we face. The practice of science, under varied social and political conditions, has become a state and/or corporate activity. The production of science and knowledge has been a byproduct of complex forces including scientists' own motives. Defining the role of science (rationalism), Feyerabend seeks to "remove obstacles intellectuals and specialists create for traditions different from their own and to prepare the removal of specialists (scientists) themselves from the life centers of society" (Feyerabend, 1978: 7).

For decades research methods and their practitioners have followed one philosophical orientation: logical empiricism or positivism which has had a dogmatic certitude. Paul Diesing, analyzing research as a social-cognitive activity, does not claim that empiricism is totally wrong: "What is wrong is the dogmatic, simplified, problem-free version that has come down on social scientists" (Diesing, 1991: xi). Diesing concludes: "Social science exists between two opposite kinds of degeneration: a value-free professionalism that lives only for publications that show off the latest techniques, and a deep social concern that uses science for propaganda" (Diesing, 1991). The reality of professional quest in search of truth and method is a fascinating journey into the realm of science. Let us, finally, reexamine our basic units of analysis—self, society, and science—in the process of professional transmutation.

If Sigmund Freud had practiced psychoanalysis and developed his theories in today's world, his conduct would have been an ideal case for a scandalously massive malpractice lawsuit against his method (Crews, 1993). Adolf Grunbaum contends that clinical validation of Freudian hypothesis is an epistemic sieve; as a means of gaining knowledge, psychoanalysis is fatally contaminated (Grunbaum, 1984; Crews, 1993: 55). Freud's theories of personality, Malcolm Macmillan demonstrates, were derived from misleading precedents, vacuous pseudophysical metaphors, and a long concatenation of mistaken inferences that could not be subjected to empirical review (Macmillan, 1991; Crews, 1993: 55). "The unknown Freud" (Crews, 1993: 55–66) appears like a master manipulator with the streak of a patriarchal evil genius. No school of thought, except Darwinism and Marxism, has influenced the understanding of human behavior as much as Freud's psychoanalysis. Indeed our conceptions of personal and social problems are colored by the outcomes of this method.

Talcott Parsons' structural-functionalism, developed as a response to the challenge of Marxism, became a general theory of society after the Second World War. In a Hobbesian vein, Parsons replaced Marx's economic determinism by his own cultural determinism with an overemphasis on a system of stability and order (Parsons, 1951). Post civil rights developments, however, left the Parsonian "system looking like a dinosaur, albeit one rather reluctant to die" (Craib, 1985: 56). New scientific developments that emphasize the role of biological endowments are indeed creating a Jurassic Park of old values and theories that die hard (Wilson, 1998). Scientism and positivistic utopias have generated systems of illusions without resolving basic issues. Violence, war, poverty, AIDS, hunger, and starvation continue to plague the humanity in spite of these scenarios of promised new deals. What has happened to the omnipotence of science, the will of the modern state in resolving the monumental failures of this civilization?

Social welfare as an institution emerged as a response to meet people's unfulfilled needs especially in the wake of exigencies of life. To maintain the system, imbalances and instabilities had to be fixed and regulated. Post-war liberalism has sought to provide for certain human needs without adequately attending to the inner contradictions of the society. A closer look at the welfare crisis will exemplify this point.

The American social welfare system exemplifies what is wrong with an ill-conceived interventive strategy. President Bill Clinton had promised to change this system, as we know it. Both conservatives and liberals agree that the system has become counterproductive. The dynamics of this failed experiment has numerous lessons for social science theorists and practitioners. Let us examine the two points of consensus:

Illegitimacy is the underlying cause of poverty, crime, and social meltdown in the inner cities. . . . When people ask where all these 16-year-old predators are coming from, one answer is chilling: from 14-year-old mothers. . . . [T]he welfare system has rewarded everything it ought to prevent and punished everything it ought to promote. (Gibbs, 1994: 27–28)

Conservatives prefer state-run orphanages as the caregivers of last resort. "Nothing could be worse than the current system," argues Robert Rector. "The current system has already pulled the family apart. The system treats having a child out of wedlock as a favored lifestyle that's deliberately subsidized by the government." Reed, the president's advisor, disagrees with the orphanage solution: "It is the kind of goofy social engineering that these same conservatives have made fun of for most of their lives," he says. "The whole point of welfare reform ought to reinforce families and a sense of parental responsibility—not to take people's children away" (Gibbs, 1994: 30). The Clinton welfare plan that sought to transform a check-writing system into a job training program for tens of thousands of single mothers was another "undeclared war against the American women" (Faludi, 1991). The expedient politics that seeks to transform motherhood—without attacking the root causes of racist violence, institutional injustice, unemployment, low self-esteem, poverty, and gender-specific objectification—is both puzzling and inhuman. Still mystifying are the prevalent phenomena of "corporate leftism" (Cloud, 1998: 70) confounded by the labyrinths of "corporate welfare" (Barlett and Steele, 1998: 36–39).

America's social meltdown, as perceived by the liberals and conservatives alike, is caused by births out of wedlock.[8] Policy scientists and governmental programs have obviously failed to solve a national crisis. Reformist proposals, confined to Dickensian poorhouses and check writing, still do not go beyond subsistence level work training. While basic issues of equality and justice remain clouded in the rhetorical debates, oppressed people continue to live with the plagues of poverty and alienation. Its racist culture, corporate-capitalist political agenda, an ambivalent national creed, and a neo-global internationalist design abysmally thwart the American social reality. A cynical outcome is corporate welfare: "During one of the most robust economic periods in our nation's history, the Federal Government has shelled out $125 billion in corporate welfare, equivalent to all the income tax paid by sixty million individuals and families" (Barlett and Steele, 1998: 38–39).

The failure of America's social welfare system has global implications especially in the wake of the decline of the social welfare state. As globalization of economy out reaches developing nations, the impact of the American system on native cultures cannot be overlooked. The transformation of Russian society from communist to capitalist state ought to be a subject of deeper analysis and reflection. "The 'gangsterization' of the economy is draining Russia's wealth, stunting its development, scaring off investors, and souring its citizens on concepts like capitalism and democratic reform," writes Candis Hughes (1994).

If development and free economy—McDonaldization as Yevtushenko calls it—means gangsterization of a superpower, its consequences for growing economies like Mexico, India, China, Korea, South Africa, and Vietnam are boundlessly alarming. The end of the Cold War is a historic opportunity to revamp global conditions especially in the developing nations. What we have is a missed opportunity. The annual Human Development Report of the United Nations is strongly critical of most United States and other foreign aid programs, saying countries that need the most help don't get it—or all they get is guns. James Gustave Speth, an American administrator with UNDP, said:

There doesn't seem to have been a fair share of this previously inter-national money captured for a new set of international priorities—poverty elimination, environmental deterioration, drug trafficking, nuclear proliferation, population, preventive development to head-off peacekeeping needs. . . . We need a global safety net for the poor. (*Advocate*, 1994: 14A)

Contemporary functional-positivist approach is fraught with interventionist strategies usually employed in system maintenance and the nation-building models. Amid diversity and conflict, there is a need for a universal approach (Mohan, 1993a). Much of social welfare technology—social work, social policy, and social development—reflects the assumptions and applications of a pretentious science that has failed to unify knowledge as a liberating experience. America, the epitome of scientific advancement and global success, has become the world's most violent developed nation.[9] It also is a divided nation (Hacker, 1992). In its study *Progress of Nations*, UNICEF said that developing nations do a better job using their resources in caring for women and children than do the United States and Europe. "Economic progress does not equal social progress," said James Grant, the director of UNICEF (*Advocate*, 1994: 2A). A recent report from President Clinton's Commission on the Future of Worker-Management Relations exposed disturbing trends about the American social reality. Labor Secretary Robert Reich said:

A society divided between the haves and have-nots or between the well educated and the poorly educated that becomes sharply divided over time cannot be a prosperous or a stable society. (Naylor, 1994: 1A)

It is instructive to see how class struggle has played out in the land of communism's nemesis. A capitalist state, for the sake of its legitimacy, strives for equality, justice, and freedom. If mass loyalty is threatened, Habermas contends, a tendency toward a legitimation crisis is established. However, the fundamental cause of the legitimation crisis, according to Habermas, is the contradiction between class interests: "In the final analysis . . . *class structure* is the source of the legitimation deficit" (Habermas, 1975: 73). America's new class war, I contend, is inherently self-defeating; it is incompatible with the goals of scientific progress and global development.

Sustainability without "bioglobalism" (Mohan, 1988: 122) and post-material praxis (Mohan, 1992) remains an incomplete manifesto of development. New social work must eschew the myopic vision of flawed assumptions, unrealistic strategies and de-developmental outcomes (Mohan, 1996b). Empowerment, enlightenment, and empathy—rather than coping, stress, and adaptation—constitute a process that is conducive to reinvent science as a liberator of the human condition. The cult of dysfunctional paradigms sustains individual and societal atavism without any hope for a better world.

Arguing against Daniel Bell's neoconservative attack on modernism as the major source of our ills, Habermas defends the ultimate significance of the modernization process in which science, morality, and art are separated into autonomous spheres, each with its own internal logic (Habermas, 1981). Modernity is an uncompleted project and so is "Habermas's enormously ambitious attempt to salvage its still emancipatory potential" (Jay, 1985: 139). The "project" of human emancipation—freedom from techno-terror and new tribalism—remains a daunting challenge for social technologies. As globalization becomes a new social reality, future experiences will be shaped by the "political rationality" of the "technological universe" (Marcuse, 1964: xvi). Human reality still has an opportunity in the transformation of Self, which, in Sartrean logic, contains the seeds of a meaningful future:

The cycle of the future is a *meaning*: in the case of Kierkegaard, it is the Self. Meaning can be defined as the future relation of the instituted to the totality of the world. . . . In other words, [individual] is that being who transforms his/[her] being into *meaning*, and through whom *meaning* comes into the world . . . [s/he] brings human temporality into the universe. *This clearly means that the foundation of History is freedom in each [person].* (Sartre, 1974: 160–161; emphasis in original)

"There are bodies of knowledge that are independent of the sciences," writes Michel Foucault, "but there is no knowledge without a particular discursive practice; and any discursive practice may be defined by the knowledge that it forms" (Foucault, 1972: 183). The science of social reality is not yet complete; knowledge of diversity and experience will enrich the sphere of human autonomy so long as "scientificity"—independent of dogmas—remains wedded to global well-being.

NOTES

This chapter is based on a paper delivered to the 27th Congress of International Association of Schools of Social Work, Amsterdam, July 11–15, 1994 (Mohan, 1996a).

1. "From the beginning, any critical theory of society is thus confronted with the problem of historical objectivity, a problem which arises at two points where the analysis implies judgements: (1) the judgement that human life is worth living, or rather can be and ought to be made worth living . . . (2) the judgement that, in a given society, specific possibilities exist for the amelioration of human life and specific ways and means of realizing these possibilities" (Marcuse, 1964: x–xi).

2. The O. J. Simpson case is "an American Tragedy" (*Time*, June 27, 1994, cover). This also is a national disgrace; how victims of domestic violence are treated in a decadent celebrity culture.

3. Arbitrary use of hierarchical authority legitimizing legalized discrimination is a common organizational practice in all scientific, academic, social, and commercial settings.

4. David Howe has attempted a framework that incorporates several paradigms within two dominant sociological traditions: (1) stability-conflict, and (2) objective-subjective. "The four paradigms define fundamentally different perspectives for the analysis of social phenomenon" (Howe, 1987: 48). The suggested exclusiveness of the two traditions—and the corresponding paradigmatic variance—is questionable, however.

5. Increasing workplace violence against authorities in power is a notable symptom of this syndrome.

6. A group of forty-two distinguished social work researchers dispute the "heuristic paradigm" (Tyson, 1992: 541–556) in defense of the "positivist" approach "toward the common goal of improved services to clients" (Grinnell, Austin, Blythe et al., 1994: 469–470). Social theory's "great divide"— between action (agency) and structure (society)—seems to characterize the nascence of social work theory.

7. Even though violence against women and children is a national epidemic, social workers' approach to this problem is belatedly expedient. Domestic violence euphemistically conceals the institutional violence of society. The politics of curricula designs and offerings furthermore compound the difficulty of teaching the dynamics of inter-personal violence in a holistic-rational manner. While courses are "spilling over [in] our school[s]" (June Gary Hopps, *U.S. News & World Report*, March 21, 1994: 97), certain pioneers remain excluded in bureaucratically rigid institutions. Cultural atavism too often destroys the essence of pedagogical innovation.

8. "There is nothing like this in history," says Daniel Patrick Moynihan, implicitly railing against the African-American family with his new diagnosis of "speciation" to "describe the impending creation of a different breed of human, one raised outside a father-mother setting" (Broder, 1994: 7B).

9. "No issue poses the need to come together more to deal with the problems we face than does the cancer of crime and violence that is eating away at the bonds that unite us as a people," contends the U.S. President in his weekly radio address. "Unless we do something about crime, we can't be really free in this country, we can't exercise the opportunities that are there for us; and our children can't inherit the American dream," he said (*Associated Press*, June 19, 1994).

3

The Professional Quest for Truth: Paradigm, Paradox, and Praxis

The Doctrine of Essence seeks to liberate knowledge from the worship of "observable facts" and from the scientific common sense that imposes this worship. Mathematical formalism abandons and prevents any critical understanding and use of facts. . . . Knowledge deals with appearances in order to get beyond them. . . . The knowledge that appearance and essence do not jibe is the beginning of truth. The mark of dialectical thinking is the ability to distinguish the essential from the apparent process of reality and to grasp their relation.

—Herbert Marcuse (1968: 145–146)

The ontology of knowledge is ridden with paradigmatic vicissitudes that obscure the symbiosis of truth and existence. A crisis of consciousness, unleashed by the paradoxical forces of the Enlightenment continues to mystify the methods and ethos of scientific inquiry. This chapter is an exegesis of certain strands that have relevance to the discursive practice of human freedom. Paradigms of knowledge and the ethos of "scientificity" (Foucault, 1972: 184) have challenged intellectuals and professionals to strive for truth in search of meanings. Modernity, despite postmodernists' pretentious claims, is an unfinished saga of reason's search for its authenticity and substance. Paul Diesing (1991), Stephan Fuchs (1992), and Jean Paul Sartre (1992) analyze a critique of knowledge, social practice, and truth here in the light of three recent books.

If "truth is an intersubjective matter," as Sartre contended in his posthumously published work (Sartre, 1992: xiv), its interpretations and meanings are bound to impact our knowledge in relationship to our ignorance. Sartre observes: "Man is the being through whom questions come into the world.... Thus man defines himself in relation to an original ignorance" (Sartre, 1992: 2). Sartre's *Truth and Existence* (Sartre, 1992) was written in 1948 under the disturbing shadows of the Cold War and the annihilating terror of nuclearism. "And so I am searching for an ethics of the present," he wrote (Sartre, 1992: xlvi). "Human-reality, in so far as it is characterized by consciousness, creates its essence through its acts; this essence is always to come.... All thought, all practical action and behavior, imply a relationship with Truth" (Sartre, 1992: xliv–xlv).

Is there a possibility of the ethics of practice which is conceived in the womb of limited knowledge? The more we know about our universe, the less we seem to know about ourselves. "The foundation of Truth," according to Sartre, "is freedom. Thus, [we] can choose non-truth. This non-truth is ignorance or lie" (Sartre, 1992: 13).

Arnold Gehlen best summarized the modern predicament, "The premises of the Enlightenment are dead; only their consequences continue on" (Habermas, 1987a: 3). As contemporaries of the young Hegelians, Habermas contends we employ communicative reason as a radical experience of subject-centered reason; he rejects the "paradigm of consciousness" in favor of his intersubjectivist paradigm of "communicative action" (Habermas, 1984; 1987). The Enlightenment can only make good its deficits by radicalized enlightenment (Habermas, 1987a: 84). The subjects of knowledge are aspects of the decentered and irrevocably desublimated human reality: "Subjectivity and intentionality are not prior to, but a function of, form of life and systems of language; they do not "constitute" the world but are themselves elements of a linguistically disclosed world," writes Thomas McCarthy (Habermas, 1987a: ix).

Theory and practice, mind and body, facts and values, and the empirical and the apriori constitute varied contexts in which we posit the structures of knowledge in relation to social reality. "Social practice," McCarthy writes, "submits the background of knowledge of the lifeworld to an 'ongoing test' across the entire spectrum of validity claims" (Habermas, 1987a: xi). The dialectic of reason is at the heart of contemporary discourse on the philosophy of practice (Diesing, 1991) in quest of professional truth (Fuchs, 1992). The hiatus of theory and practice represents a great divide in the Western tradition.

The intellectuals stand alone because of their alienating contradictions (Sartre, [1974] 1983: 255). Bertrand Russell prided himself in being described as anti-intellectual. Bergson, who did not confuse intellectualism and rationalism, is called "anti-intellectualist but not anti-rational" (Chiari, 1975: 46). Bergson, emphasizing the oneness of integrated reason, underscored intuition as the fount of humankind's altruistic impulses and principles. The search for truth and objectivity has been fraught with paradigms of conflictual orientations and specialized interests that intellectuals have sought in pursuit of self-perpetuation. The itinerary of this process has been rigorously tenuous but rewarding. The identity of social theory remains well established even though its linkages to practice remain ill conceived and underutilized. "If there is one positive and promising aspect of the decades just behind us," writes Norman Birnbaum, "it is the secularization of social theory" (Birnbaum, 1988: 90).

A quite religious positivism, or unreflective empiricism, has marked much American social thought for a good part of the century. This took on, alternately, conservative or reformist political functions, but its basic intellectual structure was unchanged. There was a substratum of reality, and empirical procedures combined with an abstract analysis on the model of the natural sciences could apprehend it directly. (Birnbaum, 1988: 90)

Polarization of paradigms led to scientism and interventionism on the one hand and activism and propaganda on the contrary. Much of professional development in sciences is an outcome of this schizophrenic search for objectivity: cognitive reality in quest of method. The problem of paradigms, as Becker construed, lies in "the Enlightenment paradox" (Becker, 1968: 360–374).

Scientism, despite its unitarian emphasis, failed to achieve universal freedom. Somewhere in this itinerary of a supposedly lofty process, intellectuals forgot their mandated role in the very society they live in and seek to serve. The angels of reason became inadvertent victims of unfounded faith. As a result of this self-imposed myopic vision, goal-displacement has gradually transformed a benign servant into a monstrous reality that has eclipsed both reason and freedom. The consequential birth of a new culture of unreason, if you will, is at the heart of civilizational malaise. Or else, how can we explain the un-intended, uncontrollable horrors of AIDS, nuclear annihilation, and ozone depletion in a world hopelessly mired in the monumental fail-ures of this century's determinist ideologies: capitalism, communism, fascism, Nazism, and fundamentalism? The fact that a Hobbesian Third Wave (Toffler and Toffler, 1993) threatens much of human-kind, the loss of innocence seems to outweigh the gains of a much-acclaimed progress. "Success is not progress," Sartre once said.

A schema for research consciousness and a professional quest for knowledge posit the two interrelated foci in a critical perspective for both theoretical and practical purposes of scientific inquiry (Diesing, 1991; Fuchs, 1992). This analysis is a critique of truth with three specific objectives: To unravel science and social reality in light of (1) philosophy of science, (2) organizational politics, and (3) the contin-uing saga of critical analysis. This "prismic" view of reality situates the units of analysis in a holographic context that is both pertinent and challenging to the nature of this discussion.

PHILOSOPHY OF SOCIAL SCIENCE: SEARCH FOR A METHOD

The relation between Reason and Practice has been a subject of debate along the idealist and naturalist traditions. Feyerabend con-tends: *Idealism* assumes that Practice (the practice of science, of art, speaking a natural language, custom as opposed to formal laws) is crude material to be formed by Reason. Practice may contain ele-ments of Reason but in an accidental and unsystematic fashion. It is the conscious and systematic application of Reason to a partly struc-tured, partly amorphous material that gives us Science, a Society worth living in, a History that can pride itself on having been made by [humans] at their best. *Naturalism*, on the other hand, assumes that history, the law, sciences are already as perfect as they can be. The attempt to rearrange science or society with some explicit the-ories of rationality in mind would disturb the delicate balance of thought, emotion, imagination, and the historical conditions under which they are applied and would create chaos, not perfection (Fey-erabend, 1978: 7).

Diesing's work, which is dedicated to Feyerabend, is intended for practicing social scientists with three specific questions: (1) What are the actual goals of the various current research methods? Call the goals "truth" or "knowledge"; then what characteristics does achieved truth have in various methods? (2) What social, cognitive, and personality processes occur or should occur during research, and how do they contribute to the outcome? (3) What persistent weakness and dangers appear in research, and what can we do about them? (Diesing, 1991: ix). For decades research methods and their practitioners have been subjected to one philosophical orientation, logical empiricism or positivism, which has had a dogmatic certitude. Diesing does not claim that empiricism is totally wrong (Diesing, 1991: xi). Analyzing research as a social-cognitive activity, Diesing unravels scientists' own conscious and unconscious motivations, socio-politico-exchanges, predilections, interests, and personality orientations as they interface research. This construct embodies the principle of reflexivity, "any knowledge of social practices is also knowledge of the practices of social scientists" (Diesing, 1991: xi). Last, the subject of truth is synthesized with a sense of realism and humility: pragmatist euphoria is a delusion and introspective appreciation of the limits of science is desirable. Diesing's analysis of philosophical approaches encompasses various fields including sociology, anthropology, psychology, economics and philosophy of science. To examine the question how social science ought to work, a range of philosophical applications from positivism to hermeneutics have been explored. His conclusion is well taken:

Social science exists between two opposite kinds of degeneration, a value-free professionalism that lives only for publications that show off the latest techniques, and a deep social concern that uses science for propaganda. (Diesing, 1991)

Between value-free professionalism and activist propaganda, there lies an abyss of reason and unfreedom which does not seem to concern Diesing. Also, an ideology-free democratic society unspoiled by science is an ontological fantasy.

The human condition, social reality, and scientific progress logically constitute a valid framework for legitimizing the authenticity of knowledge if pursuit of truth is the ultimate scientific goal. In light of this postulate, the failure and success of modernity ought to be examined as a universal project. When children die of hunger and malnutrition in the callous darkness of the post-Cold War wastelands

(Afghanistan, Angola, Somalia, Iraq, Haiti, and Rwanda), when Americans shudder with fear in the despair of inner cities and in the dazzling lights of their affluent neighborhoods, and when Kuhnian communities become tools of corporate oppression, an array of questions must be asked of all scientists, philosophers, and academics: What is the purpose of science? What has become of their mandated professional values? Is science a liberator or an organized oppressor disguised as a "false and pretentious messiah"? (Mills, 1959: 16). These questions have assumed urgency because the current settings of scientific knowledge have become the Wal-Marts of cheap ideas, Machiavellian careerism, corporate greed, and welfare. Michael Milken's appointment in the business school of the University of California at Los Angeles epitomizes the triumph of thuggery in the ivory tower of truth. The known junk-bond wizard's thievery is less worrisome, however. It is the unprincipled success of the compulsive careerist on the campus that marks the nadir of a new morality of expedience. "The higher circle" of the power elite (Mills, 1956) has permeated the innermost enclaves of our society; nowhere is this tragicomedy more visible than in a university set up where hierarchies of power—rather than the circles of study—determine the environment of research production and pedagogical discourse.

If scientific progress had followed the ethics of development in harmony with universal values, the dawn of the twenty-first century should have been pregnant with equality and justice across nations. Instead, we have a world ravaged by the horrors of new tribalism. Science has failed to educate people to think critically and responsibly. The temples of light and learning that once heralded freedom and justice have now become sanctuaries of culturally condoned corruption where self-service is an end in itself. A society cannot exist without an integrated "self" as well as a sense of community (Mohan, 1996). Lester Thurow, in his latest book, *The Future of Capitalism* (1996), writes that American society could collapse from a lack of community. A massive and widening rise of inequality in a peaceful time, Thurow argues, is a sign of incivility. Freedom appears eclipsed under the clouds of unprincipled expedience (Mohan, 1993).

The demise of dissent is a price that academia paid to placate the political centers for its own vested interests. The outcome of this perverse growth is that arrogance and ignorance mutually sustain each other in the name of a new cult of efficiency. Organizational goal-displacement is a pervasive phenomenon. Globalization of economy, especially in the shadows of a singular Superpower, has created a world map of new functional nations that overlap and define each other by a complex set of Hobbesian contours and Darwinian longitudes. Organizational politics has elevated expedience to the level of ethics and this is an unrecognized scandal of the scientific world. No wonder why "pork barrel" projects perpetuate the psychopathology of intellectual self-perpetuation. The fund-raising institutional neurosis negates the essence of academic quest.

ORGANIZATIONAL POLITICS AND PRODUCTION OF KNOWLEDGE

Fuchs' thesis posits organizational dynamics at the center of scientific enterprises. He argues that science has become the religion of modernity; the debates between conflicting paradigms are not really debates over methodology but over organizational politics (Fuchs, 1992: 2–9). As such, the power of science as the most respected and authoritative world view is based on its superior material and organizational resources, not on its superior rationality (Fuchs, 1992).

Approaching science as a social construct, Fuchs, in a rather ambitious attempt, contributes toward theories of scientific organization as well as scientific production. Models and paradigms are sketched for clarity and elucidation. Sociology of science, paradoxically, represents interdisciplinary imperialism—as Randall Collins calls it—as well as a reflexive meltdown. Fuchs looks at sciences as invisible organizations. Organizational theory has greatly contributed to our understanding of the systematic causes and effects of differences among various systems. Collins sums up Fuchs' thesis:

Sciences are organizations insofar as they are regular and repetitive networks of interactions that exhibit their own structure: denser in some places than others, turned inward toward certain common foci of attention. These invisible organizations have their own hierarchies of power; they control access to material resources such as lab equipment, jobs, journals, and book publishing. . . . Philosophical issues in the sociology of science are not free-floating; just how much relativism and self-conscious constructivism emerges is itself the product of organizational conditions found in some kinds of networks, and not in others. (Fuchs, 1992: xv–xvii)

Objectified knowledge, hermeneutic interpretations, patterns of changes through cumulation, relativistic and positivistic outcomes are products of different organizations. Unifying a neo-Durkheimian vein and the technological paradigm in organizational research, Fuchs approaches science as "a particular work organization whose technologies and social structures determine the ways in which groups of scientists do their research" (Fuchs, 1992: 7). As a new dogma, instrumental reason and technical objectivity have transformed methods into cults (Fuchs, 1992: 2). Science, "as a conflictual and stratified struggle over organizational and symbolic property" is much like "politics and social conflict" and "scientists at the work place look more like Garfinkelian sense-makers than Parsonian, Popperian, or Lakatosian rule-followers" (Fuchs, 1992: 4–7).

Production of scientific knowledge is a process in which organizational dynamics plays a significant role. The ramifications of this contextual variable are abundantly clear. The Herrnstein-Murray "Bell Curve" (Hernstein and Murray, 1994) treatise signifies how scientific method and social practice are politically entangled.

The venue of knowledge is also at issue. How free is the university system today? Bill Readings rightly contends that the university is in ruins. As a microcosm, caught in the coils of consumerism, the university has to find a new language in which to claim its role as a locus of higher education (Readings, 1996). Like the world and like knowledge, Michel Serres writes, "the university is also divided into provinces linked in a relation of domination, some having more power than others. . . . Can discovery come about in a closed group, ranged in battle order, in which all defend only their own interests?" (Serres, 1997: 10). Here, as Serres warns, we touch on the gravest danger for today's universities: the danger of losing, through provincialism, the truth of their name and the fertility that this universality promises.

THE END OF THE SYSTEM: OR, THE COMING OF DIONYSUS?

The praxis of philosophy, in the post-Nietzschean vein, deconstructs metaphysics aesthetically heralding the new mythology of Dionysus, the absent god who is coming for discourse. This Nietzschean counter-Enlightenment culture of thought—the end of philosophy—is perhaps the crux of the scientific paradox. A postmodern echo of the Hegelian logic of the "end of the history" continues to reflect in the "end of philosophy" (Rorty, 1989). The unitarian world view that has positivistically inspired a deductive, "hard," quantifiable method of research is inherently flawed to analyze and interpret the inner side of the ontological social reality. Hermeneutic science, therefore, emphasizes the validity of inductive method based on the interpretation of objective-subjective dualism. If "the current Methodenstreit has its underpinnings in organizational politics and structure," as Fuchs contends (Fuchs, 1992: 195), the whole enterprise of science ought to be subjected to a philosophy of knowledge which is not yet developed. In other words, a philosophically correct science is what we need to ensure the development of a sane anthropodicy in an insane society. Is it the climax of the Enlightenment paradox or the end of science itself?

A value-free science does not stand as an independent reality. Social reality is a symbolic construct of ontological existence. Knowledge, human interests, and objects are inseparable aspects of being. The discourse on science and knowledge with particular emphasis on the professional quest for truth must therefore focus on three imperative criteria of validity: (1) The nature of phenomenon and methods of study; (2) the social reality and its constructs; (3) the context and contents of scientific knowledge. A discursive perspective on the subject would enable the scientists and philosophers to develop their paradigms without competitive dysfunctionality which often degenerates into a counterculture of scientificity.

The false objectivism of positivists' conception is strongly refuted by Habermas's theory of knowledge-constitutive interests (Habermas, 1972). "The postulate that science could rise to pure theory through the bracketing or unmasking of positions of interest was self-deception," wrote Nikolaus Lobkowicz et al. (1972: 193–210). Positivism, to Habermas, "is the refusal of reflection and thereby the denial of that critique of knowledge which is the task of modern philosophical discussion" (Lobkowicz, 1972: 197). Habermas's critics argue that his view that the technical interest is constitutive of empirical-analytic science mistakenly presupposes an instrumentalist conception of the cognitive status of scientific theories (Keat, 1981: 73). The thesis of knowledge-constitutive interests, which critics found "as vague as its irritating" and "opaque" (Lobkowicz, 1972: 201, 205), is revisited by Habermas in *Theory and Praxis* (Habermas, 1974) with multifaceted development of his views. Karl-Otto Apel and Dietrich Bohler have further advanced Habermas's notion of "emancipatory interest" inherent in self-reflection. The intersection of reason and commitment as Habermas postulated, Apel concludes, thus cannot be treated as an accomplished feat, but at best as a "regulative principle" in the Kantian sense of the term: a pure signal for reason but without substantive connotation (Lobkowicz et al., 1972: 220).

Habermas, in his later work (Habermas, 1984; 1987), retreated from these knowledge constitutive interests though one of his colleagues continues to pursue this trend of argument (Apel, [1972] 1980; 1984). The concept of knowledge-constitutive interest became an instant anachronism (as early as 1971 with the publication of the English version *Knowledge and Human Interests*) in the transition from transcendentalism to a theory of communicative competence (Lenhardt, 1972: 244–245). Language, itself dependent upon social processes, is "also a medium of domination and social force" (Habermas, [1970] 1988: 287). Habermas's *Theory of Communicative Action* (1984) rests on the didactic nature of human interaction: We are all communicating creatures capable of conducting a dialogue. This "ideal speech situation," according to Stanley Fish (1990: 451), puts Habermas in a unwinnable fix as he cannot answer the following question:

How is one to know that a shared orientation between participants is a reflection of universal validity claims and not the claims of a local or partisan project whose sway is (at least for the moment) unchallenged? How does one know whether the pragmatic and strategic components of speech have been set aside and bracketed or have merely been concealed by the force of presupposed norm? (Fish, 1990: 453 in Kaplan, 1992: 505)

Social theory, like science, may be deemed as a political endeavor. Habermas's attempt to develop an emancipatory social theory on the model of psychoanalysis, according to Keat, involves both a misreading of Freud and a misconceived opposition to deterministic reductionism (Keat, 1981). The Nietzschean-Sartrean-Foucaultean historico-ethical position posits ideology, freedom, and truth in a neoglobally valid context that seeks to universalize liberalism as the new religion of the post-Cold War era. The world community was trying to overcome the pain of the holocaust as the Berlin Wall was falling down. But "ethnic cleansing" in Bosnia brought back the horrors of the recent past. What about the human condition in Afghanistan, Somalia, Haiti, and Rwanda? Globalization of democracy, after all, must strengthen diversity without carnage, violence, hunger, and disease. Or, is it the dawn of new barbarism when science will explain every possible malady—from infidelity to mass murders—in terms of genes? What are political and ethical ramifications of this new age for the theory and practice of science? Is the pernicious "Bell Curve" (Herrnstein and Murray, 1994) going to legitimize the atavism of cognitive power? Aren't we playing god while planning mass production of the designer babies? These are basic questions which must be rephrased for critical understanding. Critical application of science as well as social theory is both a maxim and mandate of the scientific spirit. Critical social science seeks to weld power and ideology in such a way that, in the end, "knowledge coincides with the fulfillment of the interest in liberation through knowledge" (Habermas, 1974: 9).

Professionalization of scientific knowledge ought to be praxis of development rather than a specialized endeavor of mere intervention. In social welfare, social policy, legal and medical sciences which employ a vast array of interdisciplinary orientations, practice of science assumes an extremely important role in the transformation of society. In social research and practice, one occasionally finds the fragments of a crisis-ridden anthropodicy (Epstein, 1993; Mohan, 1988; 1992; 1996a; Specht and Courtney, 1994). To underscore the logic, epistemologically, I have argued that "Social praxiology" should substitute the existing methodologies of social intervention (Mohan, 1988: 12, 21–22). Social praxis, however, ought to be grounded in aesthetico-axiological order rather than Wesleyan Methodism (Mohan, 1992; Marquardt, 1992). I have argued against the dedevelopmental aspects of professional knowledge, skills, and values (Mohan, 1996b). While some critiques predict the end of social work (Kreuger, 1997; Stoesz, 1997), I have pleaded for a new social work (Mohan, 1995; 1996b). The demise of social work, one can argue, is attributable to its own regressive ideologies, behaviors, and practices. The politics of science, euphemistically, promotes a dehumanizing civility generally surrounding race, gender, and class. The outcome is a tidal wave of "the new sovereignty" (Steele, 1992) which submerges reason in the depth of a cultish counterculture.

Authenticity of communication and purpose of knowledge, then, must decide the content and character of scientific norms and practices. Social praxis undergirds the essence of progressive social theory and practice. Richard Rorty posits Habermas as the leading nonironic liberal committed to unfettered human communication (Rorty, 1989). Habermas, like Rorty and Faucault, considers the possibility of a lib-

eral society in intersubjectivity but he is very skeptical of the twentieth-century romantic revolutionaries. The didactic aspect of human
nature—that we can understand, empathize, and tolerate each other
as communicating animals—suggest that we can give an order to values that thwart the forces of liberal democracies (Kaplan, 1992: 494–
495). The global response to the continuing crisis of the post-
industrial society is at best a failure of the expected didactic communication.

The greatest paradox of civilization is that science has become corrupt, shoddy, and inauthentic. Not only the person, but the intellectual also, is alienated from the basic ethos of scientific progress. To
Becker this "is like a haunting curse over social sciences" (Becker,
1968: 366). Becker writes:

[T]oday's intellectual is alienated exactly as was his Enlightenment prototype: he is caught in the identical bind between abstruse analyses of his
subject-matter and the impotence of his active powers. Unless we understand
this acute similarity between the Enlightenment intellectual and today's social scientist, we will not be able to understand today's drama in social science. (Becker, 1968: 367)

The scientific revolution that demythologized ossified structures of
values and old habits of thought seems to have atrophied for want of
direction that mandated human liberation as the primary objective of
progressive development. "A paradigm is what the members of a scientific community share," concludes Thomas Kuhn, and "conversely,
a scientific community consists of men who share a paradigm" (Kuhn,
[1962] 1996: 176). A bureaucratized, commercialized science under
the aegis of industrial, educational, and military sectors has become
an instrument of oppression and expression of arrogance (Mohan,
1992; 1993). "We may know more about the universe than our ancestors did," writes Vaclav Havel, "and yet it seems they knew something more essential about it than we do" (Havel, 1994: 46).

This is related to the crisis, or to the transformation, of science as the basis
of the modern conception of the world. . . . It fails to connect with the most
intrinsic nature of reality, and with natural human experience. *It is now more
a source of disintegration and doubt than the source of integration and meaning. It
produces what amounts to a state of schizophrenia: Man as an observer is becoming
completely alienated from himself as a being.* . . . The world of our experiences
seems chaotic, disconnected, confusing. There appear to be no integrating

forces, no unified meaning, no true inner understanding of phenomena in our experience of the world. (Havel, 1994: 46 emphasis added)

Reflections on social reality and practice of social science must seek to unify "self, society, and science" (Mohan, 1996a). A symbiosis of social science and public philosophy is imperative for specialization and professional growth (Bellah, Madsen, Sullivan et al., 1985: 300). The post-modern world, especially within its neoglobal thrusts, tends to perpetuate a false consciousness which, paraphrasing Herbert Marcuse, "is immune to its own falsehood" (Marcuse, 1964: 12). Demystification of postmodernity's alienated consciousness on the one hand and revival of the Enlightenment sense of values on the other, constitutes the theme of a mega project which all scientists must join to achieve universal freedom. This is the essence of unification.

NOTE

This chapter is based on my article (Mohan, 1997b).

4

Paradigms of Social Work: A Search for Unification

The science of man, then, was gradually abandoned in favor of *scientists of man*. We must allow ourselves to appreciate the full force of this subtle but serious change. The science of man was a passionate problem, put forth by committed and hopeful men. It was the big discovery of the Enlightenment, incubating to its full size in the post-Revolutionary world. It had to be approached cautiously and fervently, but it had to be plied into service for man—for man in society—for mankind as a whole. The science of man was *the new world revolution*—it was the great idea of the time. . . . I am implying that the idea of the "explosion of knowledge" in the science of man is largely a myth, a myth that serves to divert our attention from the task of organization and simplification.

—Ernest Becker (1974: 10, 15)

Paradigms, in Kuhnian terms, are "universally recognized scientific achievements that for a time provide model problems and solutions to a community of practitioners" (Kuhn, [1962] 1996: x). "The extraordinary episodes in which that shift of professional commitments occurs," writes Thomas Kuhn, "are the ones known in this essay as scientific revolutions. These are the tradition-shattering complements to the tradition-bound activity of normal science" (Kuhn, 1996: 6).

In light of the epigraph that I carefully chose for this chapter (Becker, 1974), I intend to critique the notion of scientific revolution in social science in general, social work in particular. I premise that unification of science is a revolutionary epoch in human development as modern scientists—having abandoned their primal responsibility—are collectively guilty of bad faith. A scientific devolution—rather than revolution—is currently in process.

Kuhn's structure presents history of science as a cyclic process. Paradigms, also called "common disciplinary matrix," represent periods of "normal science"—a consensus view. A crisis is imminent at the end of a particular scientific epoch when new discoveries don't correspond to the existing theories and contradictions inherent explode a prevailing view. New ideas simply add to the confusion without any resolution. Scientists begin to look at nature from a new perspective, which leads to a revolution—the "paradigm" shift.

Kuhn's metaphor of Darwinian evolution—undirected improvement, but not improvement toward anything—is regressive. Steven Weinberg correctly asserts that we need to make a progressive change in it: "the progress of physical science looks like evolution running backward" (Weinberg, 1998: 52). Weinberg illustrates:

Just as humans and other mammal species can trace their origins back to some kind of furry creature hiding from the dinosaurs in the Cretaceous period . . . in the same way we have seen the science of optics and the science of electricity and magnetism merge together in Maxwell's time into what we now call electrodynamics. . . . We hope that in the next great step forward in physics we shall see the theory of gravitation and all of the different branches of elementary particle physics flow together into a single unified theory. That is what we are working for and what we spend the taxpayers' money for. And when we have discovered this theory, it will be part of a true description of reality. (Weinberg, 1998: 52)

What we see in social sciences in general is devolution of scientific process. Social work's functionalist-positivist evolution is a counter-revolution. Nothing short of a "paradigm" shift can revolutionize this process. As a formalized professional specialty, social work has come of age. Yet, its "legitimacy crisis" seems to confound the developmental process involving disciplinarity, epistemology, and general accountability. This chapter seeks to examine these issues and offers a unitary logic for the unification of social work education, practice, and research (Mohan, 1988). The logic of a unified SW-EPR is validated by the nature of scientific inquiry and social theory that undergird the duality of social reality and social praxis as a universal paradigm. Unification is suggestive of a whole human reality without the monothetic implication of a global doctrine. Unraveling the dynamics of post-modern social reality—the dialectical symbiosis of human diversity and conflict—an alternative perspective is offered to integrate social theory and practice in a synthesized model.

The development of social work as a method and discipline is reflective of our worldview and perspective on the human condition. The intersection of human and social realities has been a valid domain of the natural and social scientists that have analyzed and interpreted social phenomenon according to their epistemology, paradigms, and methods. Specialized disciplines, however, created conceptual islands and social reality became a fractured datum. An obvious imperative has been a mindless dualism perpetuating an unscientific schism between objectivity and subjectivity. The consequence of this Cartesian dualism is: we peruse egalitarianism without scientific rationale and scientism without conscience. Social workers' pragmatic preoccupation with practice models in isolation from their epistemological constructs amounts to an inadvertent malpractice. The germs of this fatal dualism lie in the organizational compost of social work EPR that contains ambiguities of cultural heritage, paradoxes of political milieu, and anomalies of societal goals. Three premises are examined here to undergird a unified model of social work theory and practice: (1) The significance of social theory; (2) the post-modern crisis and social reality; and (3) unification of knowledge, praxis, and human development.

THE RISE AND FALL OF SOCIAL THEORY

Social theory is a product of human imagination, empirical ingenuity and universal awareness. All value-neutral endeavors apparently pursue a natural science model, which implicitly excludes valuations. Social theory, its conjectures and formulations undergird observations, facts, values, and knowledge about social phenomena that warrants inquiry, analysis, and refutation. Individual predilection and institutional bias, overtly and/or covertly, permeate the whole process of scientific inquiry. It is, therefore, imperative to qualify the intrinsic underpinnings of the scientific method. An objective evaluation of this process will enable us to appreciate the nature of social theory that constitutes the unrecognized soul of social work.

Reconceptualization of philosophical perspective is perhaps the first interdisciplinary step toward an effective and authentic methodology. Ann Weick unravels a developmental schism between the values and knowledge in social work (Weick, 1987: 218–230). By inculcating this integrated conceptual base, Weick contends, "a richer, more unified philosophical context is produced" (Weick, 1987: 218). Contemporary social welfare, social work, and social policy constitute an incongruent salad offered piecemeal in ideologically fragmented contexts (Gil, 1990: 13–63; Mohan, 1988: 61–80). A cognitive loss of the whole reality is a consequence of epistemological dissonance and ideological conflicts. The outcome of this crisis is a fragmented profession in search of an identity, an incomplete anthropodicy in quest of a paradigm, and a parasitic discipline alienated from its mission.

Social theory is a logical interpretation of varied and complex social processes, experiences, and phenomenon. Social practice bereft of this conceptual-cognitive base is both invalid and ineffective. Despite methodological excellence, specialized endeavors proffer incomplete— often-inaccurate—conjectures devoid of substance. In Plato's allegorical cave, "one can only see shadows cast on a wall by objects from an unknown source" (Reamer, 1992: 257–259). Practitioners of social science must make a unified effort to recognize social reality in its completeness. Only knowledge wedded to values, meanings, and interpretations undergird by sound theoretical constructs can deliver us from the shadows of a Platonic cave.

We perceive an object, experience a feeling or sensation, and interpret, explain, and describe their meanings to the world. This hermeneutic—interpretive, analytic, descriptive self-indulgence—realm of knowledge is an attempt to simplify an otherwise complex world. Social theory offers clues and constructs that synthesize inductive and deductive reasoning toward the understanding of this complexity.

The contours of social theory unfold a perplexing labyrinth of human-social reality. "Much modern social theory is either unintelligent, or banal, or pointless," says Ian Craib (1985: 3). Social theory is by definition general; it seeks "to explain and understand experience on the basis of other experiences and general ideas about the world" (Craib, 1985: 4, 7–8). From social action to structuralism, one notices certain "theoretical traps"—crossword puzzle, brain-teaser, logic, and description—that explain the nature and scope of social theory

(Craib, 1985: 10–13). A socially critical scientist uses data, analysis, and explanations to reconstruct—or deconstruct?—social reality. Methodology becomes a powerful tool of social transformation in the hands of policy makers, scientists, and technocrats who are engaged in the process of transmutation. Where do social workers fit into this grand design of historical social transformation?

From Immanuel Kant to Jean Paul Sartre, reason has been a focal point of philosophical investigations. Social theory, between Parsons and Habermas, has embraced the labyrinths of social action and social structure. In pursuit of knowledge, scientific inquiry has followed an objective-subjective, reflective-analytic, intellectual-intuitive duality. Social workers' uncritical acceptance of functional logic on the one hand and adherence to positivistic intervention and liberal activism on the other, has nurtured an epistemology of being which is alienated from its primal mission: universal emancipation. We are helping professionals who would go on Band-Aiding the victims of war without questioning the logic and morality of mass murder. We are practitioners of a trade which mystifies the causes of human misery, and often, blames the victims (Ryan, 1971). The myth of scientific objectivity has blinded our innate rationality to challenge the structure of evil (Becker, 1968). Social workers by purpose, persuasion, and pedigree operate independent of the culture of social theory. They use theoretical concepts without input in their production; they apply its constructs without understanding; they comprehend problems in isolation from the drama of etiological dynamics. Their application of borrowed theoretical notions is often mixed with resistance and reluctance. Their practice is thus fraught with unintended consequences of inauthenticity. A near total dependence on other social sciences for theoretical support relegates social work's position in professional hierarchy. A parasitic character raises the question of professional legitimacy. A noble, potentially universal, theodicy has unwittingly become a victim of its own professional conflicts, naivete, and hubris.

Scientific knowledge, positivistically conceived, is morally neutral; it is, however, inherently repressive because it "contributes to the maintenance of a form of society in which science is one of the resources employed for the domination of one class by another, and in which the possibilities for a radical transformation towards a more rational society are blocked and concealed," according to the critical theorists (Keat, 1981: 2). A liberating science modeled after Freudo-Marxian synthesis has not yet evolved. Functional logic muddles through the alleys of dysfunctional designs reinforcing new cults of efficiency under dubious pretexts and fustian rationale.

The search for an emancipatory paradigm remains illusive. In social welfare, a few critical social theorists have made certain dents of consequence to social policy without qualitatively impacting the modalities of practice (Epstein, 1993; 1997; Mohan 1992; 1993; 1996; Schram, 1995). A hiatus between theory and practice thus permeates the entire system. Clinical orientation and emphases in education, research, and practice subtly thwart the development of critical reasoning. The constitutive interest of social work/welfare knowledge is historically functional and pragmatic rather than emancipatory. The discursive practices of governmentally sponsored welfare research, Sanford Schram contends, "reinforces state interests about how to understand 'the poor.' " Schram writes:

Reports on welfare policy research are written in an economistic-therapeutic-managerial discourse (ETM) that imputes to the poor the identity of self-interested, utility-maximizing individuals who need to be given the right incentives so that they will change their behavior and enable the state to manage better the problems of poverty and welfare dependency. This discourse concentrates almost exclusively on disembodied information on individual behavior as the primary way to isolate causes of poverty and develop solutions.... Welfare policy research masquerades as neutral and autonomous data-confirmed knowledge, only to remain impotent when appropriated. (Schram, 1995: 4)

The fall of social theory was imminent. Disciplines that thrive on pragmatic rationale without epistemological background and commitment generally remain preoccupied with short-term issues without enduring substantial concerns. Their bodies grow fat on the junk food of expedience without any nourishment of soul. Their existence becomes a mindless pursuit in search of self-promotional endeavors— making a lot of noise signifying nothing.

THE POST-MODERN CRISIS AND A CORPUS OF KNOWLEDGE

"The fact that science cannot find any purpose to the universe does not mean there is not one," writes an essayist (Overby, 1993: 74). "We are free to construct parables for our moral edification out of the laws of the jungle, or out of the evolution and interdependence of species. But the parables we choose will only reflect the values we have already decided to enshrine" (Overby, 1993: 74). Modernity gave us a science-based civilization. It also gave us perfected artifacts of genocide, holocaust, and total annihilation. In the aftermath of the Cold War, scourges of poverty, violence, AIDS, drugs, ethnic cleansing, and bigotry are still with us. A new culture of sex, lies, and cover-ups demonstrate the decline of the world's most powerful democracy. Are we, as a human race, progressing? I have argued that development of "post-material values" (Mohan, 1992; Habermas, 1989: 252) must precede deconstruction of democracies of unfreedom (Mohan, 1996).

Social work as a profession represents an organized response of the advanced industrial society. Post-industrial problems, however, present new dimensions of age-old anomalies. On the surface, one notices cocaine babies, victims of AIDS, indigence, and homelessness in the shadows of skyscrapers. Inside the micro and macro systems, however, simmer the anxiety and avarice of an ailing society. In other words, the "poverty of affluence" (Wachtel, 1989) is a daunting challenge to the limits of our collective ingenuity. The paradox of poverty and racism in America—a country based on the creed of equality and justice—offers a rationale for new perspectives. I plead for a new social work whose discursive practice is anchored in the epistemology of human liberation.

Fundamental democratization is not an unrealistic goal in the age of democracy. The theory and practice of social work must imbibe, inculcate, and impart those values, skills, and knowledge that promote equality and justice as the guardians of human freedom. The contemporary models of practice serve cathartic-narcissistic needs of maladjusted individuals and groups without transforming their social reality: values, attitudes, and behaviors. In other words, we seek comfort in the dysfuctionality of culture without deconstructing its basic tenets.

Transformation of human reality is a function of social praxis. Social praxiology, a discipline that is not yet developed, may seek to address causes and consequences of human tragedies and social problems from a radically different perspective. At issue are three basic questions: (1) Has science universally and fundamentally improved the human condition? (2) Are human conditions outcomes of the social reality? (3) How can knowledge, values, and techniques maximize human and social development? An answer to these interdependent problems is offered in the following formulation:

Science, ideology, and pedagogy—through developmental praxes— can reconstruct social reality for self-empowerment, human-social development, and overall societal well-being. This three-dimensional conceptualization is presented in three contexts of social praxes:

Human-social/Developmental	Politico-economic/Institutional	Cognito-normative/Epistemological
Science: Autonomy/Facticity	Inquiry & Justice	Synthesis
Ideology: Self-Actualization	Liberation	Empowerment
Pedagogy: Reflexivity	Curriculum	Enlightenment

The relationship of knowledge and freedom has been problematic ever since "reason" and "intellect" began to shape the human condition. The politics of knowledge is an undeniable ingredient of social reality. The three contexts of social praxes postulated above present science, ideology, and pedagogy as facets of an intellectual process which is not always grounded in "reason." The intuitive reason is therefore crucial for context and contents. At the end of a millennium, it may not be difficult to conclude: "Society, Western society at least, repudiates systems, hierarchies, established moral canons and doctrines, and from political to aesthetic, moral and religious dogmas, throws everything into the melting-pot of re-examination" (Chiari, 1975: 188).

Social praxis rises like a phoenix from the ashes of the Western decay. A synthesis of thought and practice, aesthetics and ideology, art and science—all glued in a cycle of self-renewal. Science, says Joseph Chiari, "is bound to be stained by the human" (Chiari, 1975: 189). "Philosophical discourse, which used to rest upon reason and logic," Chiari concludes, "is now fragmented and no longer expository, descriptive or revelatory of the nature of being, but is used as a weapon of demolition so as to bring to new life new values or a Nietzschean transvaluation of values" (Chiari, 1975: 190). The eclipses of reason, civility, and freedom have apparently generated a new culture of unreason, barbarism, and unfreedom. The purpose of social theory should be to organize otherwise chaotic phenomena of social realities by critical analysis and new interpretation. The eclipse of critical theory is a consequence of triumphalism, a new hubris of

Darwinian tide promoting the ideologies of avarice, pugnacity, and globalism.

It is asserted that John Wesley was the greatest social reformer in the West "because he succeeded in bringing social-ethical theory and praxis into a close connection that served both" (Marquardt, 1992: 137). The corpus of knowledge, as Michel Foucault defined, is an outcome of unity and interconnections amongst varied discourses. Foucault writes:

In "sciences," like economics or biology, which are so controversial in character, so open to philosophical or ethical options, so exposed in certain cases to political manipulation, it is legitimate in the first instance to suppose that a certain thematic is capable of linking, and animating a group of discourses, like an organism with its own needs, its own internal force, and its own capacity for survival. (Foucault, 1972: 35)

TOWARD UNIFICATION

A responsible, humane society is a construct of reason, freedom, and civility. Unreason and unfreedom dehumanize discourses of civility. A specter of social breakdown is not a mythical conjecture. From Oklahoma to Bosnia-Herzegovina, to Russia, to Mogadishu, to Somalia, to Afghanistan, one notices the rise of a new tribal awakening that is characterized by intolerance and brutality. New primitivism has eclipsed the voices of civility. Ethnic cleansing, nationalism, and xenophobia represent a perverted rationalization of a new cult of violence which is deeply rooted in human atavism. Human behavior is still a perplexing challenge to demystify the paradoxes of modernity.

The Enlightenment served as the womb of a new age of reason. Scientific progress had implied humankind's liberation from its own trappings. Scientism, however, became a dogma of new superstitions justifying inequality and lynching. The innate power impulse—or the politics of science—turned technology into a machine of human oppression. Social work, of necessity, has become an agent of this misguided utopia. Our avowed values and professed ideals have lost their significance in the rapacious climate of neo-global forces. Social workers masquerade as agents of change without an understanding of and commitment to social transformation. This amounts to an inadvertent malpractice of reason.

Brian Appleyard decries the spiritual damage that science has caused to "the soul of modern man" (Appleyard, 1993). Timothy Ferris summarizes Appleyard's case in four points: (1) Science is essentially amoral and has no values; (2) Science is irresistible; (3) Science is thus responsible for a general and spiritual decline in Western culture; and (4) Therefore science must be resisted (Ferris, 1993: 17–19). Social work intervention is a positivistic adaptation of modern techniques, knowledge, and values without critical appraisal of social reality. The human condition thus eludes ameliorative strategies. The counterproductivity of some of our welfare programs speak volumes of the failed ideology. On the other hand, collapse of a collectivist paradise in the former Soviet Union is macrocosmization of the same behavior. The consequences of the failed culture of intervention are universally paradoxical: racism in America, genocide in Europe, violence in Gandhi's India, and poverty and starvation in humankind's native continent (Africa) collectively represent the evolutionary failure of postmodernity as a process.

In our efforts to optimize objectivity we often become unscientific. Scientific interpretations and endeavors need not exclude inter-subjectivity. In the realm of human affairs, it is inter-subjectivity that reconnects people to people, history to history, and culture to culture. We have not yet developed a language of expressing new dimensions of human diversity and oppression. On one hand we are trapped in our ethnocentric myopia, on the other hand we remain painfully anthropocentric. Modern social work is guilty of both. To demythologize the twin handicaps, one must think critically and act globally. This is warranted by realities of the new world order that cannot define itself, let alone lead us to a safer and secure future.

Social work cannot reinvent a new science but it has an obligation to develop an epistemology of its own. Unification of science is not a discovery of the wheel; it is a reaffirmation of an old universal value that upholds the cosmic unity—and dignity—of the human family. Unification of social work ought not to be misinterpreted as the integration of its diverse conceptual pluralism. It is a modest attempt to redefine the very purpose and destiny of a profession lost in the primal incompleteness of its epistemological evolution.

Social work's attempt to claim a scientific status is rather unrealistic. A professional discipline without an epistemological base of its own stands on a shaky foundation. Much of social work's scientific debates emanate from the pretensions of the empiricist-behaviorists of the 1980s. The polemics of issues involved contentions about social

work effectiveness (Fischer, 1973; Segal, 1972; Wooten, 1959), revolution (Fischer, 1981; Gordon, 1983), obsolete scientific imperatives
(Heineman, 1981; Schuerman, 1981; Geismar, 1982) and emerging
issues and related epistemological problems (Specht, 1990; Haworth,
1991; Specht and Courtney, 1994; and Epstein, 1993; 1997; Wakefield, 1993; 1995) which raise nagging debates about social work's
identity, mission, and methodology (Mohan, 1988; 1995).[1] Many
onto-ideological blind spots continue to underscore the legitimacy
crisis. How can a particular viewpoint, a single-subject design, an
evaluative study or a role-playing technique ever adequately unravel
the phenomenology of the inner city despair? Is causality so simple
and casual? The difficulty of credibly establishing the causes of social
conditions, William Epstein asserts, raises "the sticking point in almost all social welfare constructions" (Epstein, 1997: 11). "The ambiguity of cause—the essential issues of fact—together with differences over basic social values promote the factionalism of political
debate" (Epstein, 1997: 11). Harry Specht, fearing "social work is on
the verge of being engulfed by the popular psychotherapies" (Specht,
1990) eloquently surmised:

We should not be secular priests in the church of individual repair; we
should be the conscience of the community. We should not ask, "Does it
feel good?" We should help communities create good. We must have a
vision of social work that enables us to direct our energies to the creation
of healthy communities. That is how we make healthy people. (Specht, 1990:
356)

What is the central problem that we as social workers are most
concerned with? The kitsch of contemporary literature is filled with
rhetoric of varied competencies (skills), diversity, and empowerment.
Social justice, suddenly, has become the sexiest motif our new age
practitioners of ethical practice. On the surface it feels comforting
but, in reality, looking at the profession's fragmentation and self-
infatuation, it is both hypocritical and self-deluding. I see no
"tradition-shattering" evidence in sight; we are followers of "the
tradition-bound activity" (Kuhn, 1962: 6) that has guided our
journey through the twentieth century. If alienation, human oppression, and social misery are central issues of social work practice and
research, it's time to turn around and reflect on the inadequacy and
failure of conceptual frameworks and "paradigms" that define the
contours of our professional domain.

Schools of social work and agencies—the organizational settings where knowledge, values, and skills develop—are confronted with the obsolescence of leadership and vision. At times pedagogy is unrelated to the general drama of human existence. Issues unrelated to knowledge development preoccupy major resources and institutional crisis seeps into the fabric of organizational relationships. Darwinian imperatives—territoriality, pugnacity, and acquisitiveness—virtually dominate social work culture without a conscious self-awareness. A subconscious state of denial speaks volumes of collective cognitive dissonance. Structures of knowledge manufactured through such a mitigating process cannot be liberating.

Unification of social work transcends methodological, ideological, and territorial boundaries. Its purpose is to relate to the human condition as a universal whole. This premise involves the interaction of three universal elements of human existence. These fundamental elements include: (1) the transcendence of human reality as an experience; (2) pervasiveness of power as a natural impulse; and (3) universality of social praxis as a method of change. Unification of social work seeks reinvention of an epistemology that does not dichotomize facts and values, objectivity and subjectivity, and science and social justice. Such a unifying body of knowledge is a collective challenge to all practitioners of science, especially those who profess the art and science of healing, reform, and change—discursive practice. A unifying theory of social reality is yet not available. In closing, let us be reminded of Michel Foucault's words:

The analysis of discursive formations, of positivities, and knowledge in their relations with epistemological figures and with the sciences is what has been called, to distinguish it from other possible forms of the history of the sciences, the analysis of the *episteme*. This episteme may be suspected of being something like a world-view, a slice of history common to all branches of knowledge . . . it is the totality of relations that can be discovered, for a given period, between the sciences when one analyses them at the level of discursive regularities. (Foucault, 1972: 191)

NOTE

1. I do not intend to review these investigations in this chapter or anywhere else in my current or future writings. An excellent account of these research findings—sometimes loosely referred to as "paradigms"—is available elsewhere (Epstein, 1993: 63–100).

PART II

IT DOES TAKE A VILLAGE

Life on our planet would be much easier if only men and nations could live in peace. But apparently they cannot. Is this because they are unaccustomed to it? Or perhaps because they need to simplify things? For war simplifies everything by reducing the options. The gulf separating good and evil widens. On one side, everything seems just; on the other, unjust. . . . If only we could celebrate peace as our various ancestors celebrated wars . . . if only our sages and scholars together could resolve to infuse peace with the same energy and inspiration that others have put into war.

—Elie Wiesel (1990: 225–226)

The village metaphor can be extended to the human family. It is this universal context that is crucial to unraveling the nature and future of social work in the next millenium. Chapters in Part II deal with de-developmental aspects that warrant a call for new social work; define the context and contours of global social praxis; examine the issues germane to deconstructing a post-industrial society; and reflect on futuristic developments that are crucial for humankind's well-being.

5

Against De-development: Reinventing Altruism

The West and the East, though different in so many ways, are going through a single, common crisis. . . . [A]s soon as man began considering himself the source of the highest meaning in the world and the measure of everything, the world began to lose its human dimension, and man began to lose control of it. . . . I feel that this arrogant anthropocentrism of modern man, who is convinced he can know everything and bring everything under his control, is somewhere in the background of the present crisis. It seems to me that if the world is to change for the better it must start with a change in human consciousness, in the very humanness of modern man.

—Vaclav Havel (1991, 11)

REINVENTION OF ALTRUISM

In response to Clifford W. Beers, William James wrote on April 21, 1907, a letter regarding the need and feasibility of a National Society that Beers founded for the well-being of the mentally ill. James wrote:

I have never ceased to believe that such improvement is one of the most "crying" needs of civilization; and the functions of such a Society seem to me to be well drawn up by you. . . . Nowhere is there massed together as much suffering as in the asylums. Nowhere is there so much sodden routine, and fatalistic insensibility in those who have to treat it. Nowhere is an ideal treatment more costly. The officials in charge grow resigned to the conditions under which they have to labor. They cannot plead their cause as an auxiliary organization can plead it for them. Public opinion is too glad to remain ignorant. As mediator between officials, patients, and the public conscience, a society such as you sketch is absolutely required, and the sooner it gets under way the better. (Hardwick, 1963: 232–233)

The most "crying" needs of civilization have often challenged public conscience. The societal responses have varied in both kind and substance depending on the zeitgeist and historico-social context. In the early 1960s, I visited many state mental hospitals in India for my doctoral research and found the abysmal human condition at its lowest ebb (Mohan, 1963; 1972). *Titicut Follies*, in 1992, looked like a paradise compared to the horrors of the state mental hospitals that I studied in Agra, Bareilly, and Varanasi (Mohan, 1971, 1972, 1972a). The society at large looked like a slaughterhouse that dumped its human waste in abominable snake pits. I did not see any sign of public conscience then. I still do not see any ray of hope when I see homeless schizophrenics in the glittering streets of America.

Altruism is a manifestation of guilt, complacence, and anxiety. Also, it is arrogance and anthropocentrism in disguise. A responsible society devices arrangements and invests heavily in developing an institutional culture that takes care of the poor, sick, and the needy—regardless of their demographic features—on a universal basis. The welfare state was deemed to be an ideological compromise until neoconservatives, on the two sides of the Atlantic, reinvented the wheel of privatization. The Dickensinian echoes still reverberate the policy documents that failed both the people and their governments.

Can we re-invent altruism? An honest answer lies in the responses to these two questions: (1) Can we reinvent human nature? (2) Can we redefine the social?

Obviously we have two alternative paradigms: Darwinian and Marxian. Much of theoretical-scientific discourse still centers on these conflicting ideologies. The end of ideology is not the end of human nature. Our social problems remain as challenging and complex as they have been before. One can argue, as I do here, that scientific devolution has created a specter of misguided hopes that confounds the lingering evils: genocide, ethnic cleansing, racism, poverty, illiteracy, famine, hunger, and disease (not to mention the terror of biological, nuclear catastrophes). Notwithstanding the Frankfurt school, social theory offers no unifying clues to universalize the "human-social" paradox. The failure of science and its paradigms have promoted clusters of growth and pockets of development at the expense of universal well-being. Overall, this amounts to de-development—a chronic stage of optimal dysfunctionality beyond any measure of hope.

The evolution of altruism has pre-Darwinian roots. Elliott Sober and David Sloan Wilson, unraveling the psychology of unselfishness, discuss the evolutionary genesis of human behavior (Sober and Wilson, 1998). Richard Lewontin identifies three unifying themes that plague evolutionary biology today, "and all three converge in the problem of altruism that is the main subject of *Unto Others*" (Lewontin, 1998: 59–63). First, evolution is an optimizing process; second, the individual organism is the object seen directly by natural selection; and last, producing altruism to unrelated strangers is to lend fitness at interest (Lewontin, 1998). For sociobiologists, Lewontin concludes, "unselfishness is the key and all else is commentary" (Lewontin, 1998: 60).

In their view evolution occurs at many levels of causation, from the gene to the population. . . . In psychology they accept the existence of egoistic, hedonistic, and irreducibly altruistic motivations for apparently altruistic behavior. . . . They are methodological reductionists, because to ascribe actions at higher levels without an attempt to explain them at lower levels invites an indiscriminate obscurantist holism that is the enemy of understanding. (Lewontin, 1998: 63)

The crises of societal development and human behavior are interdependent to the extent we discuss "the human" and "the social" in a context. The cyclic waves of liberalism and conservatism reflect the levels of collective social guilt about the human misery. The states of welfare are in disarray. The crisis, however, is deepened by the neoconservative backlash against the promise and performance of the Great Society. A critical awareness, I contend, is a necessary imperative in any task that calls for reinvestment, renewal, and reconstruction. One can argue that professional social work is a hedonistic occupation in the service of both career and ego. Perhaps this is true of all professions. When altruistic motives merely serve as cover for selfish trappings, service oriented callings become especially vulnerable. The sordid happenings of abuse and fraud in public and private organizations are not too uncommon. The culture of each professional discipline defines the extent and magnitude of vulnerabilities that corrupt both rationality and benevolence.

I believe three dimensions, sketched below, constitute the context of professional disciplinarity, which are germane to epistemological (X) and ideological (Y) character:

a. normative-cognitive structure;

b. organizational-political climate;

c. ethno-demographic characteristics.

A, B, C of each professional endeavor is ideologically colored with obvious epistemological implications. Social work as a specialized activity has evolved along X and Y axes in differential degrees of accountability and effectiveness emphasizing caring and sharing—the two pillars of responsible society. I will explore these dimensions in a sequel to this study (Mohan, forthcoming). Suffice will be to contextualize the ethos of human-social development beyond the dualism of a dichotomous tradition.

A profession's mission is an embodiment of societal values, expectations, and scientific progress. Defining the mission is an act of commitment; its re-invention is a matter of responsibility. Professionalization of social work is a post-war development. A bruised society seeks to rehabilitate its vulnerable and adversely affected populations with preventive and restorative measures. Science, ideology, and social values come to play a complex role in the process of social transformation. Social work's identity and methodology represent some of the most puzzling issues of modern times. A field that has increasingly become Balkanized in the name of diversity, unification of method and purpose must be the primal task of a responsible community. Social work's schizophrenic-parasitic identity and a nearly chameleon character, continually raise the legitimacy question at a critical juncture. Jane Adams and Mary Richmond had two different worldviews. Existing epistemologies on human conditions are equally fraught with ideological fissures and logical contradictions. Now that most professional schools have pragmatically adopted a medical model to manufacture psychotherapeutically oriented practitioners, a few educators are asking soul-searching questions about its mission, effectiveness, and pedagogical methods. These voices of dissent and disillusion-ment—in a frying, whining culture that blames the victims, idealizes "coping and adaptation" amid pervasive injustices, and makes capital out of self-indulgence—ought to be heard and reiterated. The New-tonian "Contract with America" which was designed to dismantle the foundations of a Great Society—finally culminated into the Starr dev-olution, which trashed both democracy and its own inventors.

"If the roots of social policy lie in the social contract thesis," I wrote a decade ago, "the determinants of human behavior ought to be explored in an evolutionary framework. . . . The world realities of contemporary cultures and political systems dictate that each nation move to a progressive direction to become a dynamic whole of the universe" (Mohan, 1985: 133–34; 1985a). What we encounter today is a regression of vision and approach. At the outset of Contract with America, a *Chicago Tribune* cartoon depicted a banner that read, "The Dark Ages come to Liberal City." Newt, driven in a wooden cart pulled by a mammoth looking elephant, says: "Bring Out Your Dead Programs!" Nearby one notices a medieval office of "Ye Olde Great Society" (*Advocate*, 1995, January 15: 8B). A Hobbesian, rather than Jeffersonian, view of human reality permeates the American politics of convenience. The slayers of the evil—the big government—befit human and social realities in self-fulfilling paradigms: "us" and "they," "neat" and "weird," as Gingrich once proclaimed. The insane destruction of the Alfred P. Murrah Federal Building in Oklahoma City exploded the reactionary myth of an anti-government revolution. The evolution of "revolution" seems to have come full circle.

The New Deal and the Great Society came to symbolize the quin-tessential nobility of the American character that reflected the *zeitgeist* of universal freedom, the Rousseauean concept of human nature. The courageous programs of the Great Society—Medicare, Medicaid, and other anti-poverty programs—that its architect introduced in the late 1960s, have not yet eliminated poverty from the land, as was origi-nally intended. It is, however, hard to comprehend what this society would have been like without them. The demise of the Great Society is not an electoral accident, however. It is an outcome of a lingering legacy, an unresolved dilemma, and an unanswered question. It's a product of unprincipled pragmatism and divisive politics uncommit-ted to general social well-being. It also is a manifestation of the chi-meras of illusion and discontent. Whatever is the genesis, the demise of the Welfare State is reflective of the inadequacies of post-industrial

democracies that promoted cyber-populism without real empowerment.

Today's politics are volatile and unhappy, says Kevin Phillips, more
than they are liberal or conservative (Phillips, 1994). Propaganda,
popularity, and pragmatism have polarized people beyond the ideological boundaries. Nonetheless populism is a poor substitute for
principles. Modern politics have invented models of policies, change,
and governmental roles in the developmental processes. However,
personalities, group factions, and class interests outweigh the avowed
directions in national discourse. The collective psyche thus becomes
a mirror, rather than a generator, of a never-ending drama: a game
that politicians and people play with each other in a democratic fashion without addressing the substantial issues of inequality and injustice. Michael Kramer wrote:

Make no mistake. Upward income redistribution—leaving the less fortunate
less protected—is part of what Newt's revolution is about. . . . Millions of
Americans are only one disaster away from poverty. A divorce, an arrest, a
disabling illness can destroy a working family's financial resources. It's fine
to be charmed by Newt's revolution—some of his prescriptions deserve support—but we should think twice before we cut. "Poverty," said the ancient
futurist Aristotle, "is the parent of crime and revolution"—a wise warning
about an upheaval far different from the one Gingrich has in mind. (Kramer,
1995: 32)

While the triumphal ship of global capitalism has run aground, the
fall of Russian, Asian, and Brazilian economies is bound to shatter
our own complacence. The contemporary American problems are far
more complex than they were three decades ago. The post-industrial
society is a puzzling wasteland of promises and paradoxes. A society
that cannot insure emotional security inside homes and physical protection in the schools has, by design, assumed the imperial role of
global leadership. What happens here is bound to have repercussion
beyond the Beltway. America's liberalism failed to achieve the mission
of the Great Society because of its inherent ambivalence, illiberalism,
and contradictions. Affirmative Action—the "wedge" issue of the
1990s—is a case in point. But, "are we there yet with affirmative
action?" asked William Raspberry (1995: 7B).

Oh, yes, redraw the Louisiana map to get rid of that awful gerrymandering,
and you know what? It's goodbye Rep. Cleo Fields of Baton Rouge, hello
Rep. David Duke. (Raspberry, 1995: 7B)

The map was redrawn; as a result, America's youngest African American Congressman lost his coveted seat. A defensive social policy troubled by white guilt unleashed an era of entitlement, promises, and rhetoric that created smoke and mirrors around the famed American Dream. "This policy of compensatory deference," wrote Shelby Steele, "was driven more by the needs of those who devised it than by those it was supposed to help" (Steele, 1995: 41).

Social reform was reduced to a series of expedient devices—group preferences, quotas, set-asides, redistricting, race, and gender norming. After these devices came to a vernacular of social virtue—diversity, multiculturalism, pluralism, role models, self-esteem and the endless stream of euphemisms associated with political correctness. . . . Shame put America in great need of social redemption, but it also robbed the country of the moral authority to pursue that redemption in a principled way. How could a society that had been living by white entitlement suddenly seek redemptive social justice by asking its former victims to pursue difficult democratic principles—advancement by merit and equal and colorblind opportunity? (Steele, 1995: 41)

Specht and Courtney tried to demonstrate how "America's excessive trust in individualistic solutions to social problems has led to the abandonment of the poor in this country" (Specht and Courtney, 1994). They called for an adult education approach to helping people solve their problems. This, they contend, "will empower users of social services instead of making them dependent on psychotherapists and infantilizing them. Moreover, it will foster communality, and in the long run it will lead to a community-based system of social-care far more efficient and effective than what we have now" (Specht and Courtney, 1994: 299).

How do you foster a sense of communality in a society which has systematically destroyed its sense of "community"? Violence, drugs, and sex have plagued our schools which ought to play surrogate parents. Parents themselves are locked into their own politics of existence which allows little time for nurturing roles. Corporate welfare has finally replaced public welfare (Barlett and Steele, 1998). A lack of civility characterizes the contemporary culture. The implications of Robert Putman's "Bowling Alone" thesis are far-reaching: "Putman's point is that without a healthy supply of 'public capital,' the institutions of self-government become brittle and can easily break" (Broder, 1995: 12B). The coarsening of discourse has eroded the quality of social intercourse that blended democratic elements of a civil order. A sadistically voracious Independent Counsel's Referral has virtually novelized the pornography of the Beltway *Kama Sutra* (Office of Independent Council, 1998). America has become a Wal-Mart of adolescent fantasies—a Darwinian Disneyland where fallen angels wallow in the ruins of the "politics of being" (Mohan, 1996). Presidential dignity, value of privacy and civility has vanished in the salacious smoke of cigar jokes.

Professional flat-earthers dominate the field, observed Epstein (1993: 96). They control professional organizations and use their prowess to exclude and include people (and their views) of their choice. Their dominance is sustained by the rising tide of new tribalism and corporate fascism. The paroxysm of a narcissistic academic-professional culture that regulates the production of knowledge and inquiry makes a mockery of higher education. The ivory tower idealism, in the midst of rampant careerist corruption, is equivalent of moralizing in a sleazy world. This decadent symbiosis has "moronized the culture and obliterated the moral center of the American brain" and, simultaneously, rendered the moralizing as "the inevitable chorus of the trashiness" (Morrow, 1994–95: 158).

Academic social work is a self-alienating enterprise in the university culture that has become dysfunctional. Academic freedom, which is the womb of social and democratic seeds, is eclipsed by the forces of unfreedom (Mohan, 1993). "Reinventing the Mission" (Mohan, 1995) is a challenge that subconsciously escapes our attention; mere recognition of its notion invokes anxiety, fear, and guilt. Unless science and its allied endeavors demonstrate their unqualified commitment to human well-being, methodologies of knowledge and practice will remain obscure in their meanings and mission. Psychoanalysis, and its unexplored liberatory potential, can help us regain our collective consciousness if we recognize our own problem and perversity. The Tofflerian "Third Wave"—I hope I am wrong—will deepen the post-industrial malaise without a common awareness. If laptop is a preferable value to raising a healthy kid, who can question the logic of guns and condoms in the world of toys and texts?

The loss of innocence is a collective human tragedy. It calls for redemptive-retrospective inquiry as a prerequisite to any planned change. Redefining mission is a quintessential exercise in self-analysis. A profession that prides itself for seeking egalitarian ideals painfully betrays a sense of commitment to basic values. In the name of pragmatic, job-oriented, self-directed practice, we perpetuate unscientific orthodoxies of our times. Anytime a reflective question is raised, territorial imperatives thwart the very purpose of debate and discourse. Worse is the state of the elitist models of higher education. How do we impart a sense of social justice in an archaic setting if we are running a profit-making industry in the name of a pragmatic strategy? How can one express a difference of opinion if the leading journals are systematically regulated by a coterie of like-minded narcissists possessed with the pernicious ideologies of individual power rather than reason? The university system's new caste hierarchy rewards its own failures at the expense of truth and inquiry. Consequently, policy choices become a euphemism for a host of exclusionary practices that subvert the very mission of education. "The elite schools of social work are the servants of the field's orthodoxy and not the paladins of a noble civic culture," writes Epstein (1995: 133).

Notwithstanding the self-congratulatory effects of authors citing each other—the intellectual helium that puffs up impact scores—all of social work has not produced a single credible evaluation of the outcomes of social work interventions, even while the overwhelming majority of research tries to show that the field demonstrates an ability to cure, prevent, and rehabilitate. (Epstein, 1995: 132)

A very senior social work educator observed at the 41st Annual Program Meeting in San Diego: "The profession of social work is like a political party" (Hasan, 1995). As an organized collectivity of loosely linked interests, professional subsystems—agencies, schools, curricula, and practitioners—thrive on public confidence without constructive social change. A system that is captive of its cognitive dissonance is bound to crash. Reinvention is, therefore, an existential necessity. Our inability to perceive, feel, and think beyond our own trappings renders us ill-equipped to design a pedagogy of praxis and transformation. A particular "discursive practice" is defined by the knowledge it forms (Foucault, 1972: 183). Production of social work knowledge is in a feckless state of intellectual regression. The institutional-instinctual creatureliness seems to outweigh the primordial logic of reason. Our unawareness of this reality is primarily responsible for the *Eclipse of Freedom* (Mohan, 1993) that nurtures the seeds of oppressive de-development.

TOWARD A NEW SOCIAL WORK

It is a collective challenge to formulate an argument against the de-developmental projects that hamper social work's professional identity as a unified discipline. The twentieth century is a paradoxical juncture in the history of civilization. Historian Fritz Stern warns, "history can visit upon its victims" (Stern, 1989: 3). As we approach the new millennium, we must critically address the issues of our times with courage and conviction. Our search for a new paradigm posits social reality in a global context that is epistemologically sound.

New Challenges

I see social work at the crossroads of professional evolution. Three challenges must be faced with a sense of self-awareness and social responsibility. These challenges are ideological, instrumental, and aesthetico-epistemological in nature. Social work is a unifying discipline that embodies diversity and empowerment for the improvement of the human condition. Three aspects of academic social work seem relevant to its future:

Social work as a discipline

Academic social work is fraught with concerns of legitimacy and substance. It is incumbent upon social work community to create an environment which nourishes authenticity and the spirit of free inquiry. This may be accomplished by synthesizing theory and practice in order to build, rebuild, and build upon knowledge. In other words, we must face the legitimacy issues head on. There is a growing awareness to examine the relevance and effectiveness of these concerns in the realm of social work education, practice, and research (Epstein, 1993; Mohan, 1988; 1995; 1996a). The notion of "Unification" embodies the inherent, unexplored strengths of a profession that has long thrived on its parasitic legacy.

Mission, purpose, and accountability

Social work's identity crisis emanates from a complex mix of values and disvalues—a pedigree of contradictions. Much of de-developmental growth is an outcome of this dysfunctionality. The crisis of the welfare state symbolizes whatever went wrong in the reconstruction of a decent society. The nature and magnitude of contemporary social problems dictate that we rethink our whole business with critical self-awareness. Elisa Izquierdo, who was "let down by the system, murdered by her mom . . . symbolizes America's failure to protect its children" (*Time*, 1995).[1] As we approach the next millennium, social work will have to address issues of accountability and excellence with ultra limited resources—in an increasingly diverse, complex, and interconnected world. The challenges of a postindustrial society, however, must be faced with a sense of higher values. I believe it is in the interest of the entire academic community to embrace social justice as a collective goal. Teaching, research, and service are not only mutually enriching but symbiotic: without one the other atrophies. I, therefore, emphasize the power of pedagogy and research while unraveling social reality.

The need for professional social work is inherently negative in nature: had there been no oppression in the world, there would have been no social welfare activity. In other words, dialectically, the end of social work ought to be our unabashed collective goal. Regretfully, angels do not inhabit the planet. Individuals, groups, communities, and nations continually strive for freedom from their own unfreedom. The global situation in which we experience freedom and unfreedom is the basis of a new "post-material" approach to global development (Mohan, 1992, 1993, 1996). Human behavior, social environment, social policies, and social problems constitute varied aspects of a global project that remains incomplete for want of meaningful linkage systems (Mohan, 1980). No wonder *Unfaithful Angels* (Specht and Courtney, 1994) have become victims of their own success.

National and global interface

While local and regional issues assume priority in program planning, national and international contexts must be taken into serious consideration at every level. Schools of social work should be the centers for imparting a multifaceted strategy for achieving social justice, peace, and global welfare. It is no more enough to act locally and think internationally; it is imperative that we think critically and act globally (Mohan, 1997a). Globalization of democracy and economy offers countless opportunities for international collaboration, consultation, and interdisciplinary research. The specter of new global development challenges the traditional models of social and economic development. Conceptual ambiguity and methodologically flawed designs are not too uncommon in the fields of international and comparative social welfare. One must, however, eschew the temptation of viewing social development as the final stage of social work's professional evolution. The "international" hubris of careerist experts breeds myopic self-enhancement and Byzantium's complacency. Professional social work ought to resist the populist "punditocracy" of social development; the lucrative pastures in sight are illusions of success. Assertion of identity and domain is a perpetual quest in an increasingly competitive world. As some pundits seem to suggest, social work's identity need not be absorbed by the expanding contours of social development (Mohan, 1996b).

A new time is upon us. The nauseous aspects of social reality dictate that we solve the problems of human oppression with a "rational-humane" (Mohan, 1988) approach. While new ideological waves shift interventive emphasis, let us remain cognizant of our primordial commitment to the poor, the needy, and the oppressed. In so doing, we should always remain open to criticism and innovation. This spirit of self-renewal will help synergize diversity and praxis. If "all action is knowledge . . . and all knowledge, even intellectual knowledge, is action" (Sartre, 1992: 14–15), the epistemological basis of social work education, practice, and research stands validated in the service of humankind. To quote Sartre:

The end of History is the myth, which perpetually penetrates History and gives it a meaning. But History perpetually postpones this end. . . . In fact, all the "principles" of knowledge or of Reason are outside: they are instruments invented in their time by freedom in order to anticipate a reality that is hidden or half unveiled. (Sartre, 1992: 2, 177)

Aporias of a New Paradigm: Constructs, Values, and Rationality

In a "morally contaminated" society—to paraphrase Havel—any framework of social practice is likely to be a value-laden project. We are increasingly witnessing a value-free generation growing in the mist of post-industrial development. The Great Society that heralded a war against poverty and racism is in disarray. Cultural dysfunctionality inbreeds developmental nightmares. De-developmental projects are post-modern monstrosities that have become counterproductive in the ideological-methodological quagmires of the twentieth-century conflicts. As we approach the new millennium, reification of philosophy of practice seems to be in order.

The proposed paradigm is built upon this author's idea of crisis that social work education, practice, and research (Mohan, 1988: 61–80) confronts in search of excellence. The existing pattern of education is challenged on certain normative and epistemological grounds. Excursus on the rationality of the contemporary models is premised on the notion that social work's legitimacy and effectiveness are intermeshed issues. Three postulates are offered as a unifying groundwork:

Toward a New Social Work

1. **Theory**: Society is a human construct; humanistic pedagogical theories, tools, and methods constitute a rational basis of human-social development;

2. **Practice**: As de-developmental manifestations of human behavior and societal progress suggest, the logic of existing philosophy and methodology must be rejected in favor of emancipatory praxis;

3. **Research**: Since modernity remains an unfinished project, the myth of Enlightenment (Habermas, 1987: 106–130) entails scientists to rediscover the meanings and interpretations of the objective and the subjective in relation to truth and existence. (Sartre, 1992)

A framework built on these premises partakes of the entire body of knowledge, skills, and values that employ various methods in different but inherently related fields while serving diverse populations. The elements of new linkages that follows is offered as a rationale to rethink and de-construct the twentieth-century approaches.

Three Dimensions	Values	Disvalues
Secularization of Theory	Emancipation	Anthropocentrism

Purpose
a. Knowledge as a means of self-empowerment;
b. Pedagogical approach to learning praxis;
c. Synthesis of "objective" and "subjective."

Unification of Science	Humanization	Scientism

Method
a. Scientific analysis of the human condition;
b. Historialization of truth, reality and existence;
c. Objectification of "human expressivity." (Habermas, 1987: 76)

Transformation of Social	Progress	De-development
Reality		

Goal
a. Re-orientation: normative-ideological deconstruction;
b. Re-examination: institutional validity of status quo;
c. Re-transformation: a unified whole of "self, society, and science." (Mohan, 1996a)

The proposed three-dimensional model is proffered as a possible paradigm for a new thinking in social work education, practice, and research. The "A, B, C" of each dimension—in terms of *purpose*, *method*, and *goal*—are clearly spelled out in the context of values and disvalues that should be of concern to every professional committed to universal well-being. Implicit here is a conception of the human condition that is liberated from the ossified systems of ontogenetic orthodoxies. Without this realization, the human animal will always remain a "useless passion" (Sartre, [1953] 1966: 754). If scientific progress and knowledge mean anything in terms of human uplift, we will have to think, once again, critically and globally. The legitimacy and effectiveness of social work education will be determined by the extent to which this consciousness is permeated in the theory and practice of our knowledge, values, and methods.

NOTES

This chapter is largely based on my two articles (Mohan, 1995; 1996b).

1. Child protection is one area, for example, where caseworkers—beset by budget cuts and burnout—weigh whether to save the family or the child.

Yet that is exactly what Al Davis and the nation's 33,000 caseworkers are required to do. "When you identify yourself as a child-protective person you immediately pose a threat, not only to the children, but a threat to the person's income," says Bernadette Boozer, who works with the families on Federal Aid to Families with Dependent Children in one of the toughest housing projects in Washington (Smolowe, 1995). "But it's a lonely life as a social worker, because people have a skewed idea of what we do. They think we're baby snatchers," says Victoria Case of Shelby County, Kentucky. Yet, Jill Smolowe reports the 1993 case that has left child-welfare workers in her state embittered and defensive was just the opposite: social workers failed to snatch 22-month-old Daniel Reynolds and were subsequently charged with complicity in his murder (Smolowe, 1995: 40–41). These failures of the welfare system monumentally call into question the typical social work approach to society's mega problems: unemployment, racism, homelessness, and, above all, a staggering lack of social responsibility on the part of the individual as well as society.

6

Global Social Praxis

But there remains also the truth that every end in history necessarily contains a new beginning; this beginning is the promise,
the only "message" which the end can ever produce. Beginning,
before it becomes a historical event, is the supreme capacity of
man; politically, it is identical with man's freedom.
                                        —Hannah Arendt (1948: 478–479)

The post-Cold War calculus of international relationships posits
global social praxis in a paradoxical flux of hope and despair. This
chapter seeks to analyze the myth and reality of internationalism as
a movement of global transformation at a juncture when demise of
the Great Society appears imminent. The end of Enlightenment is
premised to symbolize the sarcophagus of a lost civilization. Postmodernity's cyber-tribal dualism and its implications for the post-
ideological praxis are at the heart of this analysis.

The alchemy of social change and ideological currents shapes and
transforms the structures of human need, social values, and societal
arrangements beyond regional and national boundaries. Globalization
of democracy, economy, and information has qualitatively impacted
the dimensions of social reality as we have known. The emerging
dimensions of a new social work represent both the end as well as a

new beginning. A post-ideological paradigm is emerging in different shapes.

CONSTRUCTS OF A POST-IDEOLOGICAL PARADIGM

A post-ideological context is relevant to analyzing the nature of contemporary need and future challenges of a relatively young profession that is deeply anchored in Judeo-Christian ethics. The tenets of Western philosophy as well as culture have had a great influence in shaping the design of the modern world. Along with globalization of science, technology, and economy, Americanism—a new American epoch—marks a new stage in the evolution of social work. With the fall of communism, feudalism, and authoritarianism—as new democracies sprout in Eastern Europe, Latin America, and in Afro-Asian countries—new structures of planning and development begin to surface a previously divided world. Not that we have resolved the ideological conflicts and achieved an ideology-free world order; a new tribalism seems to plague the post-Cold War world in ways that threaten global harmony. A post-ideological paradigm is a construct of this consciousness. The elements of this framework are summarized below.

Historializing Truth
   a. Deconstruction of social reality;
   b. Empowerement and uplift;
   c. Retransformation.

Democracy and the State
   a. Policy paradigm shift;
   b. Need assessment and resource allocation;
   c. People's reorientation and new project development.

Emancipation, Education, and Enlightenment II
   a. The oppressor within: The culture and oppression;
   b. Science, education, and social practice;
   c. Toward a free and responsible society.

The New World order is premised on the notion that our past will not be our future. This, however, is a revolutionary departure in a very optimistic direction. There are grounds for this unfounded optimism. Also, there are sound reasons to be pessimistic. If the light and darkness of the twentieth century are any indicators, we must remain cautiously optimistic. An explanatory note is in order to define the contours of this framework.

Historialization and truth essentially relate to our history both as oppressors and the oppressed. If truthful reassessment is allowed in all social analysis, we will come to a new awareness about the causes and consequences of our social problems. This realization fundamentally alters the age-old mythologies of culture of poverty and blaming the victim. Premised here is the notion that global democracy will become a reality—an experience commonly shared by all peoples in differential patterns. When Amartya Sen contends that there has never been a famine in a democratic country, he is basically identifying the nature of authoritarian evil that thwarts all manifestations of freedom.[1] Emancipatory praxis involves a revolutionary symbiosis of knowledge and uplift. Human liberation is a mega project. A country's rising social indicators cannot be the true measure of global welfare; nor can others' relative prosperity be the measure of the world's progress if more than half of the humankind is plagued by the scourges of poverty, inequality, and injustice. Implicit here is the power of emancipatory knowledge that historializes human destiny in a new context. New paradigms will sprout in the wastelands of human aspirations once social reality is deconstructed in a progressive direction.

The premise of a new beginning toward global development is postulated on the ideological failings and banality of the twentieth century "isms" that globalize violence, terror, greed, and isolation in different forms and sectors of life. The post-Cold War era is a unique juncture to think and act critically and globally. Once again, humankind is at a crossroads. "The West and the East," writes Vaclav Havel, "though different in so many ways, are going through a single, common crisis" (Havel, 1991: 10). To paraphrase philosopher Vaclav Belohradsky, "we must not let ourselves be corralled into histories written by victors" (Havel, 1991: 166).

Traditional ideologies and models of economic and social development have yet to define their global linkages and applications that address a universal whole. Economic globalization internationalizes certain elements of inter-societal exchange without addressing the consequences of imbalances in power, resources, and quality of life.

The new challenges contain the seeds of next century's problems. Global sustainability, as a mythical reality, helps developmental process without insuring the goal: global well-being. The political juggernaut—national interests, international conflicts, and alliances—globally regulates the outcomes of policies and programs that impact the human condition. Consequently, global development remains a rhetorical construct rather than a reality. To accomplish a universally measurable structure, certain outcomes of existential fulfillment must become demonstrable realities. This endeavor helps us define the parameters of new global development. This conceptual design mainly involves a discussion of three related constructs: (a) the end of Enlightenment thesis; (b) the limits of social and economic models; and (c) the three R's of global development.

The End of Enlightenment

In the Golden Age, following World War II, unprecedented growth of Western capitalism, Eric Hobsbawm writes, carried within it the seeds of its own corruption and dissolution. Without shared practices, common cultures, and collective experiences ours is a world which has lost its bearings and slid into instability and crisis (Hobsbawm, 1995). Democratization of knowledge and resources and their concentration in unregulated private sectors threaten to undermine the very institutions that the capitalist order brought about. In short, The Age of Extremes (Hobsbawm, 1995) is the story of the decline of civilization, the history of a world which has both brought to full flowering the material and cultural potential of the nineteenth century and betrayed its promise (Judt, 1995: 20).

We discuss global development in a time frame which even conservatives call "revolutionary" (Armey, 1995). The evolution of revolution is an intriguing subject; its analysis has global ramifications. If the Republican "Contract with America" meant to represent the demise of the Great Society, the domestic terrorism of Oklahoma City epitomized the End of Enlightenment. The Great Society was founded upon the spirit of the American Creed accepting inequality and poverty as the moral equivalent of grounds for war. The War Against Poverty became the post-war American response to the age old social problems of want, deprivation, hunger, and disease in the industrial world. As Reaganism brought about a new counterculture of anti-federal programs, a neo-Darwinist wave began to legitimize the meanness of spirit. What we are dealing with is a new "legitimation crisis" (Habermas, 1975).

The failure of the socialist utopia is not necessarily the ultimate triumph of capitalism. Richard Pipes isolates elements common to communism and contemporary liberalism and sounds a warning about the future of the West (Pipes, 1994). The newly found democratic revolution in Russia is in chaos. Vladimir Zhirinovsky's dangerous rhetoric and Chechen rebels' terrorism apparently resurrect a new version of "the vanished specter" (Pipes, 1994). In Western sector, NATO and the United Nations have failed to stop genocide and ethnic cleansing in the heart of Europe. Jacques Chirac's defiant declaration to resume nuclear testing was a flagrant disregard and slap in the face of 178 countries that signed the Non-Proliferation Treaty. "France's vital interests prevail over all other considerations, even of diplomatic nature," said Alain Juppe, Chirac's Prime Minister (Crary, 1995: 13A). Global sanctions against India and Pakistan, the other two self-acclaimed nuclear powers, signify the hypocrisy of the West rather than its moral high ground in the denunciation of the nuclear evil.

In the United States a new conflict is de-transforming the society and its politics. A plethora of wars—from culture war to domestic terrorism—go hand in hand creating a decivilizing climate conducive to divisive and populist democracy. As a consequence, the First and Second Amendments—the twin guardians of democratic freedom—have become instigators of counterrevolutionary unfreedom. About three hundred military militias abhor and threaten the legitimacy of the government. A hyper-democracy, ironically, has become an inadvertent tool of democratic meltdown: the homegrown bomb in Oklahoma City not only killed 168 innocent people, it savaged the constitutional structure of a civil order. The Unabomber, after throwing air travel and mail delivery into chaos with a threat to blow up a plane out of Los Angeles, said it was just "one last prank" (*Associated Press*, June 29, 1995). In Japan, the apocalyptic guru, didn't just forecast Armageddon, he planned it as "the incarnation of that implausible villain in thriller novels: a megalomaniac who marshaled money, scientific expertise, and loyal followers to act out his prophecies of doom and destruction" (Spaeth, 1995: 57). Timothy McVeigh and cult leader Shoko Asahara—the ultimate counterrevolutionaries from the world's most advanced nations—seemingly represent the End of Enlightenment.

The End of Enlightenment thesis is postulated on three sub-components which have far deeper implications than commonly understood. These notions include: (1) the positivist banality, affluence as the ultimate road to societal progress; (2) the myth of a post-Cold War peace; and (3) the unrecognized malaise of global declivity. These three interdependent conjectures formulate a motif in support of the End of Enlightenment argument. The paroxysm of forces has swept across nations like a wild fire under differential guises. Poverty, war, and intolerance coexist with anxiety, ignorance, and arrogance. Also, common men, women, and children of the world live only a disaster away almost in every country; the states of welfare have nearly succumbed to privatized megamachinery; fear, insecurity, and terror have become pervasive; communities are disintegrating as empowering milieux; traditional safety-nets have been ripped apart by structures of greed; and, decency and culture have ceased to exist as primary incubators of life, liberty, and happiness. The Age of Reason, ultimately, has evolved into an Epoch of Unreason where predatory behaviors eclipse human freedom (Mohan, 1993). This global "crisis of civility" is a complex phenomenon beyond simplistic explanations and populist strategies. Let us briefly examine the sarcophagus of a "dysfunctional civilization" (Gore, 1992: 216).

The rise and fall of science

Scientific revolution has transformed society without enhancing global human freedom. Although the winds of change have swept across nations, developing societies still languish in the throes of backwardness. While positive advancements in privileged sectors are clearly visible, basic dimensions of human misery remain unchanged. A kind of new barbarism prevails in the critique of science and its relationship with social practice. The academic left and the campus right view the human condition from two different perspectives. Paul Gross and Norman Levitt summarize the academic left and its quarrels with science:

Postmodernism is grounded in the assumption that the ideological system sustaining the cultural and material practices of Western civilization is bankrupt and on the point of collapse. . . . The traditional Marxist view that what we think of as science is really "bourgeois" science, a superstructural manifestation of the capitalist order, recurs with predictable regularity, in its own right or refurbished as the doctrine of "cultural constructivism." (Gross and Levitt, 1994: 4–5)

The radical feminists, multiculturalists, and environmentalists view science as inherently corrupt, inaccurate, and alienating (Gross and Levitt, 1994: 5). While I am in general agreement with Gross and Levitt that science is "the single aspect of Western thought and social practice that defines the Western outlook and accounts for its special position in the world" (Gross and Levitt, 1994: 5), I also believe that certain elements of Western culture have thwarted the full potentialities of science. Ideals of equality, justice, and freedom heralded by the American, French, and Bolshevik Revolutions were also Western. The hiatus between scientific and social revolutions, I contend, is an outcome of the alchemy of reason which has brought the fall of science as a vehicle of human liberation. How else can we explain the phenomena of preventable human suffering in the midst of affluence? Human liberation as a global necessity is nowhere a foundational imperative of scientific ethos which wallows in its own secular fables of empirical truth.

The end of the Cold War

From Hiroshima through Vietnam, Tom Engelhardt contends, American triumphalism disintegrated, and along with it, the cherished myth: victory over less-than-human enemy was in the American destiny (Engelhardt, 1995). Even though the Soviet Union has disintegrated and the Cold War is over, one cannot assume that the evils of war, genocide, xenophobia, and hunger have disappeared. "Today there are 37 wars going on in the world" (*Time*, 1995b: 66). The dark forces of unfreedom still plague the advanced and developing nations alike. Where as the tide of new democracies appears liberating, the lava of terror and fundamentalism is devouring every front of civility. The End of the Cold War myth attempts to "corporatize" neoglobalist expansion without dealing with the developmental aspects of the human condition. In spite of the historic opportunity to develop international linkages of consequence, free market economies have contributed to "corporate" rather than "global" welfare. Techno-rational corporatization of economy, health, and social and public services is fraught with unmitigated possibilities that are changing the classic nexus of individual-societal-state relationships.

The state—modern apparatus of "government"—is a pervasive reality impacting private and public sectors. However, the state is "en-meshed in society; in a sense, it is constituted by society, and society in turn is shaped by the state" (Held, Anderson, Gieben, et al., 1983: ix). Global technology and corporatism have fundamentally changed the nature and content of the state-society relationship leaving the alienated individual in a virtual state of cyber-destitution.

The demise of civility

Internationalization of social problems and social issues is a post-industrial experience. Refugees, drugs, sex, crime, violence, big-otry, and terrorism characterize the contemporary society as an irresponsible-pugnacious creature calling for help. Kindness, open-ness, and coherence are essential attributes of a civil order. Civilization is, however, a facade. The claws of fear, suspicion, and paranoia easily rip apart the edifice of culture that humankind needs for its survival and progress.

The "Third Wave" civilization (Toffler, 1980) is an intellectual fraud; it's a bastardization of the Hegelian dialectical materialism. As a construct and reality, the "Third Wave" ignores the debt it owes to its predecessors. Also, the dissolution of the communist state—and its transformation back into a capitalist society—is suggestive of the inadequacy of the "Third Wave" logic. If the feudal and capitalist societies—in the Marxian paradigm—culminated into the classless-ness of the communist society, which has dissolved into a post-ideological ghetto, the "end of history" (Fukuyama, 1989) is a premature and pretentious verdict on the validity of historical laws. The destiny of human evolution leaves one with unsettling feelings.

Beyond the Socio-Economic Schema

The determinists view economic and social development in isola-tion from life's basic impulses. Their narrowly constructed material view of social reality is circumscribed by the market place variables that do not adequately define the ontological subtlety of subjective-objective existence. Neither free market nor totalist economy insures maximum fulfillment of human potentials. In spite of inherent incom-patibility of interests between statist and corporate models, both are equally alienating. Also, these conflicting ideologies also collide with the universal meta-values. The fabled Decentralized Socialism of the former Federal Republic of Yugoslavia is a relic of the past. India's mixed economy and Five-Year Plans lay dead in the smoke-filled ministerial offices that have produced a monstrous free market. Capitalist transformation of post-communist economies in China, Russia, and—lately—Cuba is reinvigorating industrial growth but not without social consequences. Communism's demise is not a logical triumph of capitalism. Globally, the unresolved problems of capitalist and communist systems call for a critical awareness of utopian models of development.

A historian once wrote: "It is [easier] to lecture the Poles than to live their lives between Berlin and Moscow" (de Madariaga, 1946: 214). It is obscene to talk about Third World development without unraveling the dynamics of neocolonial subjugation and continuing saga of the oppressed cultures. Likewise, gambling based casino-welfare approach is poor reparation for the centuries of cultural genocide that the indigenous peoples have suffered. *Social Welfare with Indigenous Peoples* (Dixon and Scheurell, 1995) is reflective of a benevolent attitude at best. Human oppression is a pervasive experience. Socio-economic indicators of development do not fully unfold the saga of liberation; nor do they ever rectify sources of the primal evil.

Consumerism is a new mantra of uplift in the developing world. A false sense of progress conceals the daily horrors in the lives of the poor and powerless people. Brazilian boys are cruelly massacred in the streets of Rio. Carpet industry in India and Pakistan murderously exploits the young ones. Economic slavery flourishes in many a Middle Eastern oil-rich kingdoms where abuse of immigrant women and children is a national scandal. Racism and bigotry in most advanced countries thrive as a consequence of the Hobbesian development of these societies. The needs of rich and poor countries in a neoglobal design render the oppressed peoples in a universally vulnerable situation. Economic and social development models will have to comprehend and distinguish between the predatory and survival needs of the advanced and developing nations before embarking upon any strategy of global significance. The North-South divide is a lingering legacy of a hopelessly stratified world.

Secularization and corruption of science is one of the unintended consequences of unprincipled progress. Contemporary societies, advanced and developing, are globally interlocked in a morally illicit relationship in which instant gratification of short-term goals obscures a coherent view of world reality. The flowers of global economy are blooming in the wastelands of the post-feudal and industrial societies without any regard to the needs of a biodiverse world. Russian crime has gone international. Indeed "Russia's New Mafia" is rooted in the tsarist-communist legacy (Handelman, 1995). "MacDonaldization" of the former Soviet Union further deepened the malaise of corruption, crime, drugs, and prostitution by empowering the mob culture (Quinn-Judge, 1997: 58).

From Mexico to India, mushroom growth of multinational corporations is transforming the fabric of indigenous peoples. Yet, politically subjugated true natives—from Nordic countries to Zimbabwe—remain social policy's neglected stepchildren (Dixon and Scheurell, 1995). Politics of development has conveniently left behind sectors of humanity that cry for justice and empowerment.

False indicators of growth, consumerism, and misplaced values distort social reality. The dysfunctional elements and spectacles of industrial civilizations—horrid slums of Mexico City, Bombay, and Bangkok and the inner city chaos in America—represent the "poverty of affluence" (Wachtel, 1989). Children need the milk of humanity: open schools, caring families, and nurturing communities; drugs, sex, guns, violence, and broken homes terminally brutalize their innocence.

Economic and moral exploitation of women and children is one of the saddest outcomes of the free market ethic. Techno-economic rationality is a corporate myth that thrives at the expense of human well-being. Individuals, communities, and societies pay heavily for the multinational avarice that benefits economic elites. Partha Dasgupta thinks that the contemporary divorce between economics and ethics is particularly unfortunate (Dasgupta, 1995).

"Where women have advanced, economic growth has been steady; where women have not been allowed to be full participants, there has been stagnation," concludes a United Nations study (United Nations, 1995). Like race and class, gender empowerment ought to be a logical focus of developmental planning. Patriarchal institutions, however, thwart egalitarian development.

Civil and political liberties and respect for human rights sustain the institutional structures that promote socially and economically integrated units. The therapeutic state and its variants have legitimized mechanisms that rationalize private profit—in the name of efficiency—at the expense of public welfare. The design, dilemma, mission, and effectiveness of the welfare state represent a crisis of the industrial world in handling basic social issues (Epstein, 1993; Mishra,

1984; Mohan, 1988). While cycle of dependency and lack of motivation for work is attributed to the nature of the welfare system in industrialized nations, abuse of socialized services—free food, free public health care, for example—is mainly attributed to the rapacious character of the rich in Egypt and India (Ryan, 1995: 26).

Dasgupta, in his brilliant *An Inquiry Into Well-Being and Destitution* (1995) proposes to reconnect economic models with common sense morality. Also, he emphasizes the sacrifices that societies have made for economic development are counterproductive. In democratic India famine has been avoided but economic growth is comparatively slow and the threat of overpopulation and environmental catastrophe is overwhelming. In China, on the contrary, several man-made catastrophes have cost millions of lives but economic growth has been steady and demographic growth is not wholly out of control (Ryan, 1995: 24–25). Dasgupta's *Inquiry* also emphasizes increases in the consumption of basic needs as a form of investment with high returns in developing nations. He warns against the abuses of egalitarian land reforms and socialized health services, which endlessly benefit the privileged ones. The economist Lester Thurow recently postulated "an iron law of economic development": "No country can become rich without a century of good economic performance and a century of very slow population growth" (Lind, 1995: 112). Thurow's law has chilling implications for global development if material prosperity is determined as a consequential reward of economic growth and demographic discipline. Poor developing nations, it seems, will be devastated by internal instabilities with inescapable global implications. "Global pillage," according to Jeremy Brecher and Tim Costello, characterizes the nature of the "Global village." Unregulated global competition has forced workers, communities, and countries all over the world to reduce their environmental, social, and labor conditions in order to attract footloose corporations. Brecher and Costello conclude: a disastrous "race to the bottom" has caused mass unemployment, loss of income, mass layoffs, cutbacks in public services, deteriorating working conditions, devastation of small farms, businesses, and the environment, and the subversion of democratic processes (Brecher and Costello, 1994).

In the United States of America some conservative leaders who unabashedly demonize governmental intervention in the interest of free enterprise recently raised the issue of corporate responsibility.

Robert Dole said: "When you debase America, debase society, there ought to be a line drawn" (Broder, 1995a: 10B). The line of demarcation between public good and private greed is arbitrarily drawn by the politics of opportunism. Hollywood makes money; so do the NRA and private sector. David Broder rightly raises a question:

Where is the outcry from conservatives about compensation policies that have enriched the top 1 percent of Americans mightily in the last 20 years, while earnings of most working-class and middle-class workers have stagnated or declined? . . . And where were the cries of conscience last year when the minority of businesses that provide no health insurance for workers helped block the bill that would have made such coverage universal? (Broder, 1995a: 10B)

Cyberliberalism propels the duality of corporate freedom and neo-tribal banality at the same time. Conservative crusade against the "nightmares of depravity," as Robert Dole calls it (*Time*, 1995a, June 12: 26), is both opportunistic and hypocritical. John Edgar Wideman writes:

So it's not accidental that politicians reaffirm the doublespeak and hypocrisy of America's pretensions to democracy. Let's deregulate everything; let the marketplace rule. Except when rap music captures a lion's share of the multi-billion dollar music market. Then, in the name of decency and family values, we're duty bound to regulate it. On the other hand, in areas of economy where black people are appallingly under-represented—the good jobs, for instance, that enable folks to maintain families—we should abhor intervention because it's no fair (Wideman, 1995: 33).

A society that thrives on gore, greed, and gratification often finds scapegoats to conceal its archaic anxieties. Globally, the national instincts are acted out in hypocritical treaties and business deals that repudiate the avowed humanitarian goals. The impotence of the United Nations in resolving world conflicts and the growth of clandestine terrorist organizations that endanger civility is largely attributed to inconsistencies and contradictions in the policies and practices of the powerful nations. There is something very primitive about human ingenuity. When pedophiles infiltrate cyberspace, the megabyte millennium loses its romantic appeal and predatory impulses assume a vile character.

The real threat confronting the United States in the next century is neither Balkanization along racial lines nor moral decline as conservatives fear. The danger is a "Brazilian" division of races along class lines—a racial caste society with whites on the top and blacks and other dark-complexioned people at the bottom, contends Michael Lind (1994). "Brazilification" is dividing the country between the privileged and underprivileged (Coupland, 1991; Page, 1995: 7B). There is trouble in paradise: Americans are working harder, getting nowhere. "I feel lost," says Terri Yates, "Now everything goes up but people's wages. Either you're rich or poor" (Gibbs, 1995: 17). Yates represents commoners' universal saga for survival unresolved by hollow triumphallism.

Technological advancements and communications are powerful catalysts of change. Cyberspace activists—armed with computers, modems, and Internet accounts—are waging propaganda wars on the authoritarian regimes of Asia and the Middle East. "The Burmese regime has gotten away with so much because they control the information," said Strider, the pseudonymous moderator of the BurmaNet electronic mailing list. "They can't do that any more" (Peck, 1995: 19A). The impact of the information superhighway is not always benign, however. Like a double-edged sword, it cuts both ways. Words and their meanings transform the world. Communication process can significantly change their impact. In an emotional address, Bill Clinton said the power of words was greater than ever before in the information age, for both good and ill:

The communications revolution gives words not only the power to lift up and liberate [but also] the power to divide and destroy as never before . . . to darken our spirits and weaken our resolve. (*Associated Press*, 1995)

The Reality and Rhetoric of Global Praxis

Global praxis—a mega-project of social transformation involving human fulfillment and common well-being beyond the traditional ideologies of national triumphalism and/or global domination—poses a daunting challenge to national psyches and interests. The antecedents of human behavior and governmentality do not suggest an optimistic future for the emergence of a bioglobally diverse, nondeterministic New World order. This may, however, be the only escape from the crisis of the "eschatology of the impersonal" (Vaclav Belohradsky in Havel, 1991: 165).

World summits, like the Great Seven (G-7), annually ritualize business agendas that have little relevance to global well-being. Did any one raise a serious concern about the world poverty in Halifax or thereafter? The world's richest nations have failed to do anything substantial about Bosnia and Rowanda. This insensitivity of affluence is a pathetic demonstration of post-industrial narcissism. I believe it's a universal declaration of civilizational decay and decadence.

In *Rethinking Social Development*, the World Summit held in Copenhagen, globally conscious contributors discussed thoughtful issues that help define the *zeitgeist* of global development: The future of the state (Eric Hobsbawm); community and tribalization (Amitai Etzioni); economic growth and political freedom (Ralf Dahrendorf); the origins of the idea of social and economic security (Emma Rothschild); the social costs of modernization (Johan Galtung); the self-image of Russian intelligentsia (Tatyana Tolstaya); the national ideal in Africa (Wole Soyinka); and women in Islam (Fatema Mernissi) (*The New York Review of Books*, 1995: 29). The contents of the Summit Issue Papers unfold staggering facts (United Nations, 1995a). "Poverty and inequality remain and appear to be worsening" (A/CONF.166/PC/6; UN, 1995a: DPI//15888/SOC/CON—95.93084). Heads of State and Government from every region in the world collectively endorsed three core issues that will determine the quality of life into the next century. These are the eradication of poverty, productive employment and the reduction of unemployment, and social integration (United Nations, 1995a). Globalization of social, human, and economic issues helps secularize the theory and practice of developmental ideals, policies, and programs. Global development, it seems, is emerging as a viable concept out of the postmodern debris left behind in the ruins of the post-industrial society.

This new awareness is crucial to "post-material praxis" (Mohan, 1992; 1993). New Global Development is conceptualized as a bio-global movement of peace, equality, and justice; its realm transcends interdisciplinary linkages as it seeks to synthesize theory and practice, rights and responsibilities, past and present, politics and ethics, public and private, and ideological and scientific endeavors of all individuals and societies toward a world free from archaic mythologies of dogmatic thought. It is an argument and a basis for thinking, feeling, and living globally. Once the basic motifs of human reality are qualitatively transformed, structures and arrangements of existence will significantly improve. A world devoid of fear (of crime, illness, hunger), insecurity (social, economic, political, and ethnic) and violence (of poverty and injustice) is not a utopian ideal after the grim realities of holocaust, world wars, famines, ethnic cleansing, and whatever is left in the aftermath of a Cold War legacy. This post-material consciousness precedes new global development.

If Somalia, Rowanda, and Pakistan are failures of the so-called Third World, Bosnia is the "slaughterhouse" of the Western ideals and traditions (Rieff, 1995). If Indian democracy is a failure in terms of its directive principles of state policy, Western democracies, especially the United States of America, are bastions of the "barbarism of reason" (Horowitz and Maley, 1994) which problemetize politics and rationality in a free society. As the postmortem of the Oklahoma City disaster unravels, many scenarios of social malaise are unfolding. Some militia groups believe the United Nations is part of a "New World Order" that plans to take over America and—using UN troops—deprive U.S. citizens of their rights and freedoms (*Parade Magazine*, 1995: 15). A group of defense lawyers was suing the Texan factories that manufactured the explosive fertilizers. While the President castigated the hate-mongers on radio talk shows, the Wall Street described it as "echoes of Oxford," a delayed repercussion of Bill Clinton's lawlessness (Wills, 1995: 6B). The root causes of a tragedy, however, remain obscure in the obsessive national exhaustion of the O. J. Simpson trial. Finally, Monicagate and the Starr Report established the lowest new standards of sense and civility. This is hardly a reflection of the country's state of sound reasoning. We play to the chimeras of hate and terror to enjoy our freedoms but inadvertently become their victims on the self-destructive road to unfreedom. The Clinton-Lewinski scandal furthermore underlines the irrationality of a self-indulgent culture which has implications for global well-being.

NEW DIRECTIONS

Global development is post-modernity's quest for both survival and redemption. The crisis of modernity left humankind with unmitigated consequences of incomplete knowledge and a potentially abusive science. Postmaterial consciousness thus seeks the essence of subjective—objective interfaces that can harmonize inter- and intra-societal interactions without dysfunctional consequences of deterministic models. Since progress seems to be elusive despite scientific advancements, search for new directions must continue in the interest of authentic development. The premise for such an alternative cannot be gainsaid in a world where one billion people suffer the pain and humiliation inflicted by the scourges of poverty.

I believe three intertwined directions are crucial to demystify the myth and reality of global development. These elements include:

a. Internationalization of a common creed;

b. Demystification of post-modern mythologies;

c. Universalization of knowledge.

Toward a Common Creed

Twentieth century ideas—or isms—of global change, history suggests, have twice produced totalitarian scenarios of world domination (Arendt, 1948: 460–479). Unless an alternative course is reinvented, humanity's fate is tragically sealed. The need for a common creed emanates from politico-existential necessities of contemporary global culture. If capitalism has acclaimed universal accolades in post-communist era and globalization of economy is a veritable reality, one must constructively think and act upon the models of development that democratic and authoritarian governments devised in the translation of their manifested goals. Unprincipled adherence to pragmatic strategies may yield sectorial success in selected areas without significantly changing the quality of life for the general public. Corporatization of basic services leaves people without power; privatization, similarly, absolves society from its responsibility to commit itself to public welfare. It is nonsense to call social responsibility "a euphemism for personal irresponsibility" (Armey, 1995; Broder, 1995b: 9B). A sense of responsibility—personal and social—develops in a social context. Corporate civic responsibility is an oxymoron. Without social commitment, privatization amounts to a regressive approach where societal devolution grants individual a Darwinian fate. Since global capitalism has brought globalization of economy as well as technology, the post-industrial society cannot be left without a common code of conduct. Internet communications may be a boon but raunchy, online erotica—cyberporn—is a new manifestation of

postmodern necrophilia. The sad part is: it is ubiquitous and pervasive. In an eighteen-month study, "the Carnegie Mellon researchers
found 917,410 sexually explicit pictures, short stories, and film clips
online" (Elmer-Dewitt, 1995: 40). The most popular subject in cyberspace, Ellen Goodman writes, "is not philosophy or physics. It's
sex. . . . New tech, same old anxieties. Not to mention neurosis"
(Goodman, 1995: 7B). About the general ethics of business, Pope
John Paul II has written:

Profit is a regulator of the life of a business, but it is not the only one; other
human and moral factors must also be considered, which, in the long term,
are at least equally important for the life of a business. (Broder, 1995a: 10B)

Demystification of the New Cult

Cultist thinking muffles reason and suffocates freedom of choice.
Three different cults have played havoc with humanity in recent history: personality, tradition, and science. Ideology and utopia became
instruments of totalitarian social transformation embarking upon holistic social engineering without grasping the essence of human freedom. "The age of extremes" (Hobsbawm, 1995) cannot be the age
of reason, civility, and justice—the cornerstones of a "rational-
humane" society (Mohan, 1988). Hunger, poverty, and disease today,
I premise, do not pose the greatest threat to society; it's the intellectual arrogance and ignorance that has failed humanity. Global development calls for employment of scientific knowledge in the improvement of the human condition with courage, vision, and humility.

Universalization of Knowledge

Aesthetico-secular application of science, technology, and interpretations of human behavior offer problem-solving clues to ameliorate
massive global miseries. Universalization of knowledge seeks to deconstruct new structures of thought that impart pedagogical use of
developmental processes. Famine, squalor, and bigotry are intolerable
human conditions. What we need is a tolerant, humane, and global
view to deal with these problems. As past experience suggests, ideological arrogance has often resulted into authoritarian designs without
addressing the primal human issues. New global praxis is a call for a
common creed that universalizes secularism of ideas, ethics, and prac-

tices. As "conscience of humanity," scientists and intellectuals must behave globally with a sense of commitment, responsibility, and humility. In this manner, to quote Vaclav Havel, "[T]hey foster tolerance, struggle against evil and violence, promote human rights, and argue for their indivisibility" (Havel, 1995: 36).

Yes, it is true that society, the world, the universe—being itself—is a deeply mysterious phenomenon, held together by billions of mysterious interconnections. Knowing all this and humbly accepting it is one thing; but the arrogant belief that humanity, or the human spirit or reason, can grasp and describe the world in its entirety and derive from this description a vision of its improvement—that is something else altogether. (Havel, 1995: 36)

Empowerment of the oppressed—socially, politically, economically, and spiritually—is a global task of all enlightened people. By definition intellectuals, regardless of their specialties and background, are bound together within a social contract that gives meaning to knowledge and science: Human and social development transcend Darwinian and Marxian paradigms beyond natural and historical laws. Diversity, freedom, and justice—the three pillars of universal well-being—define the context and content of new global development. The anomalies of the forces of darkness (totalitarianism, imperialism, and racism) reassures a passage different from the horrors of the recent past. Science cannot be disinvented but reinventing the mission (Mohan, 1995) is a functional necessity.

Postmodernity's cyber-tribal duality is pregnant with the perils of post-Enlightenment promises. Unless hyper democracies eschew their neo-tribal trappings, global corporatization is bound to impact the sovereignty of modern states. Our contemporary culture war, trade war, caste war, and, last but not the least, info-war, pervert the class war that is not yet fully resolved. "Brazilianization" (Lind, 1994) of American society cannot be prevented if rising inequality is not addressed. The developing nations—the have-nots of the world—are rising from a post-colonial syndrome. The Post-Cold War "crystallization"—to paraphrase Gehlen (1963: 321; Habermas, 1987: 3)—of the Western nations is both myopic and short lived. Lech Walesa's old friend Rev. Henry Jankowski, in an anti-Semitic sermon, blamed Jews for Nazism and Communism. He said Poles should no longer tolerate "governments made up of people who fail to declare whether they come from Moscow or Israel. The Star of David is implicated in swastika as well in as the hammer and sickle" (Kulig, 1995: 12A). Alber Makashov, a retired general and a lawmaker, blamed Russia's problems on "zhidy," or "yids," in his anti-Semitic speech (Dolgov, 1998: 12A). The ominous dangers of global tribalism, conflict, recession, environmental catastrophe, and the persistence of the age old evils—poverty, hunger, pestilence, disease, want, and bigotry—loom large on the fate of humankind. It is doubtful whether the next century will be any less violent and rapacious than the twentieth has been. One hopes, however, that humanity's new anarchism will survive its "counter-Enlightenment" (Habermas, 1987: 5)—the desublimated triumph of post-modern ingenuity.

NOTES

This chapter is largely based on my paper delivered to the Conference on "International Social Welfare in a Changing World," The University of Calgary, Alberta, Canada, July 29–August 1, 1995, published in *International Social Work*, 1997, 40, 4: 433–450 as "Toward New Global Development."

1. Lecture delivered at George Warren Brown School of Social Work, Washington University, St. Louis, MO, September 20, 1995.

7

Deconstructing a Post-Industrial Society

I have chosen to stress an egalitarian and democratic collectivist reform of gray capitalism because I wish to resist the siren song of New Age political and social thinking, promising altered consciousness within an unchanged political economy. The chaos and disarray of international capital render such fatalism absurd and give us reason to believe that a new hour of reckoning is at hand.

—Robin Blackburn (1998: 46)

While "freedom shock"[1] has paralyzed the post-communist Russia, the Western triumphalism seems muffled by the state of a society "poised on the brink of self-destruction."[2] In the labyrinths of post-industrial development, life across nations is still mired in the banality of new and age-old problems: AIDS, poverty, unemployment, inequality, corruption, lassitude, war, crime, intolerance, and bigotry. Deconstruction of a post-industrial society partakes of a challenging significance in the post-Cold War era because a society built on the twin pillars of humankind does not yet know reason and justice. This chapter, therefore, examines aesthetico-axiological aspects of new global welfare which has relevance to the future of social/global development, models of policy, practice, and research as applicable to national and international spheres.

"History is a capricious creature. It depends who writes it," said Mikhail Gorbachev (*Time*, 1996: 62). Global welfare, in a new World Order, is a construct of post-ideological consciousness. The specter of freedom has unleashed new challenges and opportunities that call for analysis, understanding, and action. A world devoid of violence, injustice, and poverty should not sound utopian at the threshold of a new millennium. Nonetheless, global well-being is a distant dream marred by the realities of a troublesome past. Our past is a mirror of our future.

Any discussion on post-industrial society posits human-social reality and ideology in an evaluative-critical context. Industrial revolution that unleashed mass production, colonial, and eventually global economy left individuals in a society that seems to have lost its soul. The rise and fall of the Welfare State is a monumental twentieth-century event. Aspects and issues relevant to global welfare constitute important planks of a civil order. The way societies across nations design the delivery of basic human services—and relate to each other in conducting human affairs—will eventually determine the outcome of the new World Order ideology. Three basic premises underline the idea of global welfare:

1. Post-industrial problems are complex de-developmental issues; their dynamics have global implications (Mohan, 1996b);
2. Improvement of the human condition is a global challenge and industrially advanced democracies have a primary role in the alleviation of world miseries without absolving the developing world of its primary obligation; and
3. Post-material consciousness precedes global development (Mohan, 1992; 1993).

This chapter is an attempt to conceptualize the crisis and challenges of the post-industrial society. Implicit here is a notion of global welfare that is enshrined in the letter and spirit of the Universal Declaration of Human Rights.

TOWARD A JUST SOCIETY

The idea of a just society is basically a design of socio-economic justice that would promote freedom at the expense of post-industrial dysfunctionalities. Civility is a construct that is fundamentally grounded in the ethics of fairness and equality. This situates the aesthetico-axiological basis of social and economic justice in a bio-global context. Global welfare is an ancient but nebulous concept. Poets and philosophers had long espoused the idea of a "universal family" (Vasudheva kutamb-kam[3]) until modernity invented its own versions of civility.

Western democracies confront the most serious challenge in restoring the legitimacy of the Welfare State. Liberal policies and programs that supported the individuals, families, and communities are under attack by the neoconservative forces. While governments debate new ideas, growing inequality and injustice seem to eclipse human freedom (Mohan, 1993). Revisionists are critical of the ideals of a Great Society in the United States. Socialist ideals have become taboos in the aftermath of the demise of the Soviet Union. Since liberalism is a dirty word in contemporary intellectual culture, the crisis of ideas seems more lethal than poverty and injustice.

BEYOND DEMOCRACY

Democracy is process to achieving freedom. If politics of interests, party factions, and competing ideologies become a barrier in achieving general well-being, one must pause and think critically. A responsible society is a good society that values diversity, social justice, and freedom. The forces of reaction, greed, and authoritarianism have generated a climate that is fundamentally hostile to democratic principles. *Democracies of Unfreedom* challenge human ingenuity (Mohan, 1996). Unless there is an unabashed commitment to social and economic justice, a society is neither free nor democratic.

Globalization of democracy, economy, and freedom is a relatively new event in world history. A politically correct history of people's strife is not yet written. New versions of democratic practices are shaping the future of post-industrial societies. While Western democracies struggle to combat growing unemployment, inequality, crime, and alienation emerging democracies are facing uphill challenges in grasping the meaning of freedom. A taxi driver in Yaroslavl best describes the "freedom shock" in Russia: "People have no concept of freedom. They substitute freedom of action for freedom of thought. They see freedom as license" (Kramer, 1996: 51). The transformation of postcommunist society into a democratic one is an arduous and uncertain process fraught with in-built cultural impediments. Alexander Solzhenitsyn succinctly describes today's Russia:

The system that governs us is a combination of the old *nomenklatura*, the sharks of finance, false democrats and the KGB. I cannot call this democracy . . . and we do not know in which direction it will develop. (Kramer, 1996: 57)

The dissolution of the former USSR is a textbook example how systems implode within their own contradictions. The post-communist Russia, however, is no response to the decadence of the old communist system. Yuri Zarakhovich writes:

The land is going from under our feet; our world is crumbling; and we react only by hoarding salt, sugar, and matches. The people berate yet another failed leader and look for a strongman to deliver them. . . . If our leaders are liars, it is because we the people take lying for granted. . . . But we received our freedom as a gift from our masters' hands. . . . This is Russia's historical mistake, and it goes back to Peter the Great. He admired Western factories and ships, but he never saw the spiritual and cultural forces behind them. This mistake has shaped Russia's destiny down to this time. Both sausage and freedom were imported into Russia rather than attained indigenously. (Zarakhovich, 1998: 76)

If imported democracies fail, new models of policy and practice are bound to be counterproductive. Yet, there is quintessential universalism in the very concept of freedom. By implication, new and liberated nations will have to devise policy models that are unconducive to the regressive forces of oppression. However, eschewing innate atavism will always remain a challenge to civility.

Disintegration of the former Yugoslavia and the continued crisis in the Balkan states is a grim reminder. Other facets of globalization are visible in different forms in China, India, and Brazil. Can we call these countries really free and democratic? Much of the Afro-Asian world is deeply steeped in the post-colonial strife. In many countries modernization is still far away. On the contrary, the tide of fundamentalism has put progress in a regressive mode. Considering the collapse of Asian economies and chaos in Africa, Latin America, and Mexico, one has to conclude that the International Monetary Fund "is a failed institution" (Sanders, 1998: 15B). Bernie Sanders has a point:

Our goal must be to help develop sustainable and stable economies in countries throughout the world, not boom or bust processes designed to make foreign investors rich. Our goal must be to make the United States an ally of working people and defender of the poor and hungry, not a representative of the rich, the powerful and the corrupt. (Sanders, 1998: 15B)

Social development is a challenging project in a complex world. The challenge is to recognize the ultimate value of *humanizing the system* (Mohan, 1992). The Human Development Report issued annually by the United Nations Development Program features a Human Development Index that ranks countries by a combination of thee factors: average income, educational attainment, and life expectancy. These rankings represent Amrtya Sen's powerful logic: annual income growth is not enough to achieve development. Jeffrey Sachs succinctly summarizes Sen's recent contributions and recognition:

Societies must pay attention to social goals as well, always leaning toward their most vulnerable citizens, and overcoming deep-rooted biases to invest in the health and well-being of girls as well as boys. In a world in which 1.5 billion people subsist on less than $1 a day, this Nobel Prize can be not just a celebration of a wonderful scholar but also a clarion call to attend to the urgent needs and hopes of the world's poor. (Sachs, 1998: 69)

The industrial epoch was a product of science, technology, and reason. Knowledge of social development has to be ontologized, or else its practice would remain unrelated to the essence of life.

GLOBAL DEVELOPMENT: BEING AND ANTHROPOCENTRISM

Material advancements, important as they are, neither insure progress nor do they guarantee human well-being. The magnitude and nature of social problems in advanced nations testify to the authenticity of this observation. Human existence (being) is a perennial search for truth and its meanings. The "intersubjectivity" of truth (Sartre, 1992: xiv) has profound implications for the idea of universal social justice. For example, review the most recent wars—from Vietnam to the Gulf—and critique George Bush's notion of a new World Order. "When a peasant falls in the ricefield, mown down by a machine gun, we are all struck," wrote Sartre ([1974] 1983: 83).

Being, according to Sartrean epistemology, is revealed "across all human history;" and, "judgement is an interdividual phenomenon" (Sartre, 1992: xiv). The ethics of global well-being thus assumes a historical significance:

a) Man must seek being, but through historialization. His lot is historialization toward *being*. Being is the *idea* . . .

b) Authenticity must be sought in historialization. The end of history is the myth, which perpetually penetrates history and gives it a meaning. But history perpetually postpones this end. (Sartre, 1992: 2)

Our knowledge of us is the defining paradigm of human reality. Positivism, however, presents reality beyond human consciousness. Says Sartre:

To consider that the unknowable and the unverifiable fall outside of man: this is positivism. Man is being without relationship to what he cannot know. Man is defined by what he *can* know. . . . He defines what he is and what he seeks in terms of it. (Sartre, 1992:2)

Positivist-functionalist logic has created a social world that is heavily dependent on the faltering Welfare State. No wonder why poverty and racism continue to plague the conscience of the world's most advanced nation. The ethics of being, on the other hand, calls for collective obligation to end genocide, xenophobia, homelessness, and widespread misery in the developing nations. The "third world" is a lingering post-colonial legacy.

Science and technology have radically changed human relationships, spirit, and conduct. Scientism and positivism have enhanced the boundaries of hope without self-fulfillment. This hollow progress is a crisis of modernity that the contemporary theoreticians of social development have ignored. I emphasize "post-material praxis" in the process of social transformation (Mohan, 1997a). Vaclav Havel despises modernity's arrogant anthropocentrism (Havel, 1991: 11). He says:

Reflecting on that crisis should be the starting point for every attempt to think through a better alternative. . . . I feel that this arrogant anthropocentrism of modern man, who is convinced he can know everything and bring every thing under his control, is somewhere in the background of the present crisis. . . . He must discover again, within himself, a deeper sense of responsibility toward the world, which means responsibility toward something higher than himself. Modern science has realized this . . . but it cannot find a remedy. (Havel, 1991: 10–11)

The crisis of post-industrial development lies in the cultic determinism of thought. Human commitment to "something higher than himself" has eclipsed the transcendental quality of progress. Despite the rhetoric and reality of globalization, the East-West/North-South paradigm is still intact in the polemics of a painfully divided world. Advancement and success do not insure progress and well-being. The new corporate culture is globally changing social norms, behaviors and structures and its impersonal-rapacious nature has little to offer to "something higher than [itself]." The dialectic of development is thus fraught with self-alienating elements. Sartrean dialectic moves from individual *praxis*, the act of what Sartre calls "the practical organism," to the *practico-inert*, the movement, generated by human response to human need which perpetuates itself as inhuman and anti-human (Sartre, [1960] 1976; Grene, 1973: 187). Marjorie Grene sums it up:

It is out of this fall of *praxis* into its inertial consequences that Sartre sees arising what he calls "collectivities." In terms of the abstract dialectic of the practico-inert class also belongs to this category of collectivities. In industrial society, for example, it is obvious that the machine, external to the worker, organizes him from outside himself. And, by and large, the materials we work up to fulfill our needs revenge themselves by imposing a mechanical quality, a non-human organizing principle, by which its nature undermines our freedom. It is this external relation which determines class, as it does other "serialities." (Grene, 1973: 188–189)

Industrial society is an alienating phenomenon (Marcuse, 1964). The new "class" is under the impact of other post-industrial influences: media, information, ethnicity, and multi-national corporations which have compounded individual's working relationships. Corporate downsizing on the one hand and record-breaking profits on the other signify the diminishing value of "person" in a neoglobal-corporate culture. Global economy thrives on concentrations of poverty in the ghetto and the Third World sweatshops.[4] We decry developing nations for their inability to develop a civic culture (Epstein, 1994) without loathing the fact that our own "inner" cities mock the very concept of civilization. The "end of equality" (Kaus, 1992) is no comfort to the poor and oppressed who perpetually bear the brunt of savage inequalities.[5]

CONCLUSION: THE APORIAS OF DIONYSIAN LOGIC

Postmodernity's strife is a paradoxical evolution of civility itself. Friedrich Nietzsche, in his *The Genealogy of Morals*, comments that the "actual causes of a thing's origin and its eventual uses, the manner of its incorporation into a system of purposes, are worlds apart. . . . All pragmatic purposes are simply symbols of the fact that a will to power has implanted its own sense of function in those less powerful" (Nietzsche, 1956: 209–10). Nietzschean insight affords us a view of society that harbors bourgeois civility. Modernity's nihilism is a prelude to Nietzsche's Dionysian messianism which has inspired much of the postmodern discourse. Is the new god coming? Has reason brought enlightenment? Has science proved to be a liberator?

The new World Order is an other incomplete chapter of the "new age." If modernity is "an Unfinished Project," as Habermas contends (1987: xix), postmodernity's course has not yet unraveled. Postindustrial society is an extended culmination of modernity's imperfections. Continued civil strife, unresolved social issues, nagging social problems, and reemergence of old barbarism are aspects of a new tribal culture that is deeply rooted in the archaeology of human behavior (Mohan, 1993). Our monumental failures to resolve intra-societal conflicts and international tensions in a civil manner underscore the legitimization crisis of the modern state. Post-Enlightenment phase is still pregnant with unborn issues. Art, aesthetics, ideology, science, politics, medicine, surplus production, AIDS, hunger, and genocide depict human conditions in a rather surrealistic design that sometimes betrays rationality. Is it the advent of counter-reason?

The structure of postindustrial unfreedom can be analyzed by unraveling the cumulative impact of three intermeshed forces that continue to plague civilization: (1) The continued strife for human freedom and the prevailing forces of oppression; (2) poverty and inequality as global-structural issues; and (3) new tribalism that retards the goal and purpose of progress.

The total impact of the forces of oppression, inequality, and new tribalism thwarts humanity's last opportunity to revamp its state of a chaotic order. A search for order amidst chaos has long been human-kind's saga of emancipation from innate and external evils. Ontogenesis and phylogenesis explain the dual forces of evil at work. "If there is a class which has nothing to lose but its chains, the chains that bind us are self-imposed," writes Norman Brown (1959: 252). Despite the horrors of the twentieth century, there is ethnographic and anthropological evidence that proves that war and inequality predate civilization. Lawrence Keeley in his *War Before Civilization* (Keeley, 1996) finds that modern-states generally enjoy a far lower chance of being involved in a war or homicide than those who dwell in Mumford's Eden. With due recognition of the Hobbesian nature of the contemporary culture, Keely concludes that "the only practical prospect for universal peace must be more civilization" and to attain this goal "we should strive to create the largest social, economic, and political units possible, *ideally one encompassing the whole world*" (Keeley, 1996; Gourevitch, 1996: 96; emphasis added). Unless a new strategy is universally accepted, global development will not become a viable reality. The counter-Enlightenment and its potentially abusive anthropodicy have come to symbolize the sarcophagus of a lost civilization. Postmodernity's cyber-tribal dualism and its implications for global welfare have been discussed elsewhere (Mohan, 1997; 1997a).

The myth of Dionysus is a self-fulfilling prophecy. The old gods have failed and coming of the new one is a self-fulfilling notion. The only hope to achieving a new civilization lies in the possibility of dealing with chimeras of our decadent past and uninspiring present. Real progress should go beyond surface; it must substantially improve the human condition. Burning of black churches, desecration of synagogues, and demolition of temples and mosques is "more sinister than conspiracy."[6] Coexistence of slavery and corporate expansion is a postindustrial tragedy.[7] A world where one billion people suffer from poverty cannot promote a civic culture that is conducive to progress. The third world's failure to rise from its tormented past is equally unsettling.[8] Projected horrors of demographic explosion, AIDS and homelessness merely deepen the gravity of this dark social reality.[9] Do we still "fashion unfreedom as a bribe for self-perpetuation?" (Becker, 1975: 51).[10]

NOTES

1. Yuli Guzman's expression (Kramer, 1996: 51).

2. Evangelist Billy Graham decried the self-destructive nature of the society on his receipt of the Congressional Gold Medal (*Associated Press*, 1996: 3A).

3. An ancient Vedic (Hindu) concept.

4. William Julius Wilson's findings emphasize "sweeping changes in the global economy that pulled low-skilled industrial jobs out of the inner city, the flight from the ghetto of its most stable residents for a better life elsewhere and the lingering effects of past discrimination" as the main causes of "concentrated poverty" that conventional governmental programs could not ameliorate (*Time*, 1996a: 56). Nancy Gibbs, on the other hand, writes about American celebrities and companies that take advantage of the misery in the Third World: "How much are we willing to sacrifice the children of other countries to give our children what they want?" (Gibbs, 1996: 28–30).

5. More than one-third of all America's children (5.6 million) live in working families. They are part of a growing segment of American society that challenges the image of childhood poverty as caused mainly by unemployed teenage mothers, according to a study by the Annie E. Casey Foundation. "Although many factors put children at risk, nothing predicts bad outcomes for a kid more powerfully than growing up poor," said Douglas Nelson, executive director of the Casey Foundation (Douston, 1996: 1A).

6. "The prospect of conspiracy is a chilling thing," Assistant Attorney General Deval L. Patrick said. "But the prospect that these are separate acts of racism is even worse. . . . [A]n epidemic of individual terrorism . . . is tougher as a social problem" (Sniffen, 1996: 10A).

7. Sam Cotton's article, "The Silence of African Slavery," in the *New York Post* exposed the reality of African slavery (Hentoff, 1996: 7B). On the other hand, solar panels made in the United States are becoming popular in developing countries. From India and Indonesia to Mexico and Brazil, writes Julie Halpert, these solar panels are "sprouting on thousand roofs, lighting up jungles, deserts, and other hard-to-wire areas. . . . [They] are also bringing communication links, powering up cellular phones as a wireless substitute for an installed infrastructure" (Halpert, 1996: C1).

8. "Romantic notions of third world cultures are themselves barriers to change" (Epstein, 1994: 107–137).

9. A report from the United Nations Program on HIV/AIDS paints a picture of past and continuing tragedy for sub-Saharan Africa. Nearly 13 million adults in African countries are affected with HIV. That's 65 percent of the world total (Tyson, 1996: 1D). Projections say more than half of humanity will be residents of cities, those centers of commerce, creativity and squalor where, 100 years ago, only one person in forty lived. "Human

settlements will be the real challenge of the twenty-first century," says Arcot Ramachandran at the United Nations City Summit in Istanbul. The United Nations estimates 100 million people worldwide are homeless and one billion live in inadequate housing (Hanley, 1996: 12B).

10. This chapter is largely based on my paper "New global welfare: Excursus on postindustrial development," delivered to the eighth International Conference on Socio-Economics, University of Geneva, Geneva, Switzerland, 12–14 July 1996 (*New Global Development: Journal of International & Comparative Social Welfare*, 1996, XII: 1–10).

8

Social Work: The End or a New Beginning?

What remains irreducible to any deconstruction, what remains as undeconstructible as the possibility itself of deconstruction, is, perhaps, a certain experience of the emancipatory promise; it is perhaps even the formality of a structural messianism, a messianism without religion, even a messianic without messianism, an idea of justice—which we distinguish from law or right and even from human rights—and an idea of democracy—which we distinguish from its current concept and from its determined predicates today.

—Jacques Derrida (1994)

"The time is out of joint. The world is going badly. It is worn but its wear no longer counts. . . . What is happening is happening to age itself, it strikes a blow at the teleological order of history. What is coming, in which the untimely appears, is happening to time but it does not happen in time," writes Jacques Derrida (1994: 77). One is tempted to be euphoric at the end of the most paradoxical century. The specters of history, however, remind us of human banality and its singularity that transform one epoch into another without a meaningful change.

"It is a question of explicitly and systematically posing the problem of the status of discourse which borrows from a heritage the resources necessary for the deconstruction of that heritage itself," wrote Derrida in 1966 about what subsequently became deconstruction (Derrida, 1991: viii). A future is a product of its past; yet, it is not exactly the same. The shape and events of the future may be determined by the forces of its past but it remains fiercely independent of its endowments.

The future of social work depends on the future of social justice as a concept and a construct that hold together the edifice of a civil society. The world, at the end of a millennium, is about to enter a new era which is markedly different than we have known. Yet, the human condition is not going to experience a qualitative change in the realm of its existence. The continued duality of hope and despair, thus, warrants a dispassionate-critical analysis for human well-being. This concluding chapter is more than an argument against "the end of social work" thesis (Kreuger, 1997; Stoesz, 1997); it is, in fact, a reaffirmation of the ideals and practice of democracy, diversity, and social justice—the three basic concepts that legitimize the logic of discursive practice, an alternative paradigm. Implicit here is a premise that the crisis of democracy is a daunting challenge for any emancipatory praxis (Mohan, 1996).

Again, I raise a question: What is the ultimate goal of social work? Dialectically, a true answer is: The end of social work itself. Implicit here is a notion that social work is about to eradicate all social miseries and when we succeed, social work will no more be needed. The debate, however, is couched in the realties of an incomplete profession, which is uncertain of itself. It is therefore imperative to reflect on the state of social practice—its mission, methods, and relevance— in a fast changing world at the end of the twentieth century. Futuristic scenarios are inherently fraught with self-fulfilling prophecies, precognitive ambiguities and imperfections of measuring standards. A post-ideological review is, therefore, in order to:

• Analyze the state of the present human condition and social reality that warrant a particular mode of social transformation;

• Assess the epistemology of social justice that would promote discursive practice; and,

• Articulate a viable set of values and parameters—paradigm, if you will— that define the future of our profession beyond the ideological mist of twentieth century.

The discussion that follows is suggestive of an approach that may well constitute the focus of a futuristic-idealistic debate in light of the contemporary realities.

MILLENNIUM ANGST AND THE HUMAN REALITY

The millennium celebrations are filled with excitement and anxieties with an underlying impulse of nervousness about the unknown. As a rationalist one must question the "millennial madness" which is devoid of one's capacity to learn from history (Gould, 1998). At the end of the last century many enlightened people thought that the discovery of scientific methods had indeed found the Holy Grail of knowledge and the Enlightenment would lead to a paradise devoid of unwanted misery and scourges of social malaise. As "the world of oppression" (Mohan, 1993) reveals, we have not yet crossed our Jordan.

The continued strife for survival as well as a predatory lust for power and control suggests that Hobbes, Darwin, and Freud are not yet dead. The new tribalism—from Bosnia to Tiananmen Square—is suggestive of a new authoritarian stride that defies any ideological model. Ethnic cleansing is genocide; so is brutal repression of the Tibetan culture. But, the New World order does not seem to recognize the malignant resurgence of the old habits of the human animal in perplexing postmodern behaviors. While capitalism flourishes under Chinese statism, socialism is buried under the dead weight of its founders in Russia. Democratic socialism as espoused by some Western democracies and India has become an oxymoronic reality in the new orthodoxy of globalization. The rise of this new authoritarian-capitalist global culture has far reaching consequences for the practice of social work. Internationalizing social work (Mohan, 1988: 78–80) is a piecemeal measure of democratic movement. Unless individual-societal relationships can serve as vehicles of human freedoms—transforming institutional oppression into liberating experiences—no measure of mundane success can be accepted as genuine praxes. At issue is the centrality of human dignity in a decent society.

We are at the threshold of a new era. A new anarchy is upon us. Joan Dejean draws an unexpected connection between the culture wars of Ancients and Moderns in late seventeenth century France and the culture wars affecting curricular canons and national cohesion in the late twentieth century United States (Dejean, 1997). A mood of decline and fall is a common experience. A sense of *fin de siècle*, Dejean argues, emanated from this cultural crisis. Today, we are in the throes of a global cultural war, which is markedly different from its infamous predecessors.

An UNRISD study reports on the "States of Disarray" analyzing the world's major social problems and the social cost of globalization and world politics (UNRISD, 1998). The three ubiquitous forces of global oppression—rise of social inequality, moral meltdown, and cultural terrorism—seem to have destroyed the romance of life. This postulate is validated by the experiences of the oppressed people who continue to languish in the shadows of developmental paradoxes. It is a sad commentary on the rise of the post-industrial society that corporate abuse has become a pervasive reality (Wright and Smye, 1996). Workplace "is becoming uncivilized," conclude Lesley Wright and Marti Smye (1996: 3).

Other imperatives that impact the future of the human condition and social arrangements include: digital revolution, individualism, violence, and anxiety (DIVA). The DIVA of global capitalism is bound to unleash a neoDarwinian era that Adam Smith could never have imagined. "We are no longer" Keynesians either (Ohmae, 1995: 42). Nation states, Kenichi Ohmae argues, have ceased to exist in the global economy of the post-cold war era. The four I's—investment, industry, information, and individual consumers—have virtually demolished the structure of the central authority. "The only hope," Ohmae argues, "is to reverse the postfeudal, centralizing tendencies of the modern era and allow—or better, encourage—the economic pendulum to swing away from nations and back toward regions" (Ohmae, 1995: 142).

"If the present looks so grim, why does the past look better?" asks John Taft (1989: 275) "Fear of political entropy has ever been a concern of American elites" (Taft, 1989: 276). Marking an end, or a new beginning, is an arbitrary choice of preferred conditions, interests, and values. At issue is the state of the human condition at a particular juncture. What have we as a civilization achieved and lost over the last hundred years? There is so much to be proud of that even volumes cannot do justice. By the same token, the losses have been formidable. No encyclopedia can adequately document the horrors of concentration and labor camps. Oppression suffered by people in dif-

ferent ages under different dogmas and dictators serve as chilling re-
minders that civility and decency are universally noble attributes
which ought to be guarded, perpetually and freely, to avoid the darkness of dissolution, death, and destruction.

Symbolically, social work represents the American crisis of identity
and confidence. "Are we a nation?" asks Michael Lind (1995a). "Are
we a profession?" Social workers have been answering this question
over the decades. Polemics of diversity, identity, and public welfare
have commonly occupied a central place in the democratic experiences of both. Since America's future looks secure and unchallenged,
one can deduct a positive outcome about the future of social work,
which, professionally speaking, is an American innovation. A responsible answer calls for a deeper analysis, however.

"Forgetting about eternity, and replacing knowledge of the ante-
cedently real with hope for the contingent future, is not easy,"
thoughtfully observes Richard Rorty (1998: 19). The ideals of social
democracy and economic justice, Rorty, among others, thinks long
antedated Marxism, "and would have made much more headway had
'Marxism-Leninism' never been invented" (Rorty, 1998: 42).

THE FUTURE OF SOCIAL JUSTICE

Before the imperialist era, there was no such thing as world politics, and
without it, the totalitarian claim to global rule would not have made sense.
During this period, the nation-state system proved incapable of either de-
vising new rules for the handling of foreign affairs that had become global
affairs or enforcing a Pax Romana on the rest of the world. Its political
narrowness and shortsightedness ended in the disaster of totalitarianism,
whose unprecedented horrors have overshadowed the ominous events and
the even more ominous mentality of the preceding period. (Arendt, 1948:
xxi)

"No matter how much we may be capable of learning from the
past, it will not enable us to know the future," writes Hannah Arendt,
concluding her Preface to Part Two: Imperialism (Arendt, 1948: xxii).
A new, almost invisible and invincible, imperialism is with us. The
DIVA-syndrome, if I could say so, is a neoglobalist design which is
inherently dehumanizing and repressive. While it creates a new class
of the rich, it deepens the gulf between the poor and the rich, north
and south, advanced and developing nations. The "end of equality"

(Kaus, 1992) is a pernicious declaration of the "end of history" (Fukuyama, 1989) for both are allies in their rationalized defense of systemic inequality. The subtext of these theoretical, often-self-fulfilling, formulations is that the future of real equality is both bleak and uncertain. This bodes ill for the future of social justice.

Social Justice Consciousness (SJC) is the being of twenty-first century social work. Social justice is not a new construct. As long as injustice has been in consciousness, voices against oppression and inequality have raised the banner of social justice. Constitutional safeguards, however, reflect a modern approach to achieve the ends of justice without bloodshed. The success and failure of constitutional measures may be seen as the yardstick to judging the feasibility of democratic governments. At a juncture when global democracy has become a movement, it is pertinent to scrutinize the policies and results of national programs that are designed to eliminate social and economic oppression. The lack of a minimally acceptable performance standard is a pessimistic indicator. It is indeed doubtful if capitalist democracies are designed to achieve a just social order based on equality and justice. To quote Mickey Kaus:

You cannot have capitalism without "selfishness," or even "greed," because they are what make the system work. You can't have capitalism and material equality, because capitalism is constantly generating extremes of *inequality* as some individuals strike it rich—and use their success as the basis for still further riches—while others fail and fall on hard times. (Kaus, 1992: 9)

The decline of three public institutions—the draft, the school, and public spaces—is responsible for the rise of inequality, according to Kaus (1992). "Much of today's social inequality," he argues, "derives from neither money differences nor 'merit' differences, but from breakdown of public sphere institutions (like the draft and the school) that one discouraged the translation of those differences into inegalitarian attitudes" (Kaus, 1992: 181). Public institutions, however, reflect societal values and changing mores. Their decline is a statement on the failure of the civil culture that maintains segregated schools and desolate inner cities at the expense of egalitarian conditions. A society based on contradictions cannot promote equality and decency. Can we ensure social justice without guaranteeing social equality? Simplified answers are likely to compound the complexity of this question. Also, paradigmy approaches will generate different models. John Rawls and Amartya Sen notwithstanding (Sen, 1992), formulae for just and equitable distribution of wealth, privilege, and opportunities are expressions of varied class interests. If equality, justice, and fairness are noble values, then one must be an unabashed crusader against the age-old evils: injustice and inequality that breed and nurture unfreedoms. The ultimate truth is: without equality there is no justice. If inequality is an integral part of the global economy, then democratization seems to be an ineffective vehicle to combat ubiquitous injustices. Post-cold war cynicism even glorifies rapaciousness by saying: "greed is good" for success. But, the fundamental issue is: Is it progress? Is it justifiable on any moral and ethical grounds?

Rebuilding post-war economy may not be easier but it can be managed as the Marshall Plan demonstrated in Europe. War-torn societies pose daunting challenges (Carbonnier, 1998). It may be said that societal progress tends to outlive the progress of the nation. As nation states are challenged by the rise of techno-economico-regional forces (Ohmae, 1995), it is imperative that social structures eschew the regressive temptations. Failure to recognize this will only lead to new tribalism. In other words, societal forces conducive to promote social justice are more important than building and expanding national borders. The demise of the USSR and Yugoslavia offer textbook lessons to those who find solace in their complacent non-disintegration. I have argued against de-development in Chapter Five and elsewhere (Mohan, 1996b).

TOWARD DISCURSIVE PRACTICE

But William James thought that [Henry] Adams' diagnosis of the First Gilded Age as a symptom of irreversible moral and political decline was merely perverse. . . . For James, disgust with American hypocrisy and self-deception was pointless unless accompanied by an effort to give America reason to be proud of itself in the future. . . . "Democracy," James wrote, "is a kind of religion, and we are bound not to admit its failure. Faith and utopias are the noblest exercise of human reason, and no one with a spark of reason in him will sit down fatalistically before the croaker's picture." (Rorty, 1998: 9)

Uncritical acceptance of and adherence to an unrealistic "faith" becomes a dogma, which requires cultish fellowship. This is exactly what has become of certain social science models in general. As James surmised, I have offered numerous alternative frameworks in addition to constructive criticism but the Establishmentarian agents have devised a hideously one-dimensional system which screens and presents a particular kind of orthodoxy. Demise of dissent is the greatest tragedy of the American educational system. At Lucknow University, India, I could write a letter to the editor against the Vice Chancellor in *The Hindustan Times* without losing any of my faculty privileges. In the United States, it is almost unthinkable to exercise this freedom of expression without fear of persecution. The university zealously maintains an archaic hierarchical system that dwarfs the rigidity of the Indian caste system. Likewise, professional organizations pamper and patronize people, programs and policies that suit their systemic needs unrelated to their intrinsic mission. The outcome is a professional culture which smacks of racism, sexism, ageism, bigotry, and a kind of fundamentalism that is inherently antithetical to the purpose and values of social work. As I experience the reality, a new McCarthyism is in practice, which legitimizes exclusionary policies, rewarding the perpetrators of injustice for brutalizing the powerless people of color.

Models, paradigms, and frameworks are products of epistemologies and politics of a particular profession. Knowledge does not grow in a vacuum. Social work knowledge and skills that educators profess to impart and practice is guided by the politics of academia as well as social services which serve as the incubators of effective practice. The very notion of effective practice is usually determined by measures that lack scientific validity. The organization of social work as a system is patterned in a manner that suits a corporate model without its efficiency. The outcome is an ineffective, often dysfunctional, delivery of curricular objectives and services at the expense of the needy people's fate.

The contemporary practice of social work is largely patterned on Cartesian dualism. As biogenetics develop, clinical practice will no more need social workers because lab-technicians will handle all aspects of behavior and human development. John Searle concludes: "The correct approach, which we are still only groping toward in the cognitive sciences, is to forget about the obsolete Cartesian categories and keep reminding ourselves that the brain is a biological organ, like any other, and consciousness is as much a biological process as digestion or photosynthesis" (Searle, 1997: 50). Since most behavioral problems will fall in the high-tech area, the problems of soul—morality, equality, and justice—will continue to remain in the realm of socio-political discourse.

The notion of "discursive practice" is grounded in liberatory praxis which, as an abstraction, denotes knowledge for human empowerment. Social work's legitimacy as a profession is validated by standards that measure up to an accepted level of criteria. Beyond the accreditation standards, there are norms and values which all professionals adhere to as good citizens. The expected outcome is a professional milieu where one can develop and transform the cognitive and affective objectives into a repertoire of tools and values used in real life practice. A system plagued by Cartesian duality cannot be an engine of holistic transformation. Dysfunctional settings produce dysfunctional outputs. It is unrealistic to expect otherwise. Corporate oligarchy of the entrepreneurial organizations furthermore deepens the crisis of conscience. The present-day social work breeds mediocrity and narcissism that promote a dysfunctional culture. Despite feedback, the system perpetuates its own kind in varied subtle and overt forms without any awareness of a self-destructive impulse. The crisis of social work is an unrecognized reality; our collective cognitive dissonance is an unfortunate development. A crisis, which emanates from cultural, political, organizational, and epistemological reasons, ought to lead to new pathways for alternative models to avoid the paroxysm of an endemic malignancy. The constructs of a proposed "three 'C's' model of discursive discourse" are proffered below for further review and discussion.

Context

1. Altruism, attitudes, and academic freedom;

2. A profession in search of an identity;

3. A therapeutic culture that promotes cultural dysfunctionality;

The Crux

4. Definition (re-definition) and demystification of existing concepts including diversity and dissent;

5. "Historialize" societal epochs, events, and situations in search of truth (Sartre, 1992) and promote SJC;

6. De-utopianization of science (a bioglobal strategy of development; Mohan, 1988: 122–125);

Contents

7. Historico-transcendental unities of discourse; scientificity in a system of dispersion, continuity, and discontinuity; and, a new history of linkages and interconnections—horizontal and vertical—between unitary systems and transformation (Foucault, 1972);

8. Discursive dialogue and liberatory social praxis (Mohan, 1992);

9. Knowledge and human emancipation (Mohan, 1993; 1999; forthcoming; Sartre, 1992).

"Human emancipation remains a challenging and distant goal. Humankind's trilemma, at the threshold of the twenty-first century, is uniquely complex: techno-scientific progress, spiritual hollowness, and an insane arms race endanger the survival of universal humanity that has hardly recovered from some of its historical maladies"; I wrote these words about thirteen years ago when the Soviet Union and the Berlin Wall were menacing realties of the post-World War era (Mohan, 1985: 1). The world has changed yet the echo of these words resounds in our consciousness.

The three constructs of discursive practice spelled out above involve nine elements that call for unification, synthesis, and humanization toward a "bioglobal" world (Mohan, 1992). I have written extensively on varied planks and postulates of this stance but a synthesis of this framework is now in order.

In *context* is a premise that academic freedom promotes proper attitudes that foster the seeds of altruism. Caring and helping are central themes in social work. How can we achieve these without compromising professional ethics? It is the professional context that is relevant to achieving these goals. Implicit here is a dilemma that is often encountered in the means-end relationships. Expedience and effectiveness models tend to over emphasize results (outcomes) without critically examining the "means-end" dyad. Our culture wars simply aggravate a *fin de siècle* (Dejean, 1997). Our universities are in a state of chaos (Readings, 1996; Lucas, 1996; Kerman, 1997). The politics of academia is both ideological and pragmatic. However, we must eschew the temptations of expedient means regardless of the ends. Impure means do not justify noble ends. In other word, unprincipled success and careerism do not serve, let alone promote, equity and fairness leading to social justice. Leaders obsessed with careerist goals sacrifice every finer value to attain material success. When societal values become corrupt, narcissistic behaviors overwhelm. A perverse cultural milieu inbreeds the authoritarian personality which is detrimental to both human and social development. The "success" of a narcissistic-authoritarian manipulator is no model to emulate. Deification of self-serving models is a nadir of professional perversity.

Defining the crux of the problem is the most difficult task in any problem-solving process. In a diverse society people hold different interests and points of view. Constructive engagement of "deviant" approaches is not only democratic but also prudent. Dissent is the essence of democratic freedom. Discursive dialogue is an efficacious as well as empowering method. Our unwillingness to dialogue with a perceived or real adversary is an admission of undeserved guilt. Also, it forecloses possibilities of nonviolent resolution of conflict. Diehards seldom see the wisdom of acceding to a divergent view. Since prevail they must at all costs, pearls of nobility are lost in the suffocating dust of ego duels between delusional power and threatening divergence. It is inclusion, understanding, and empathy rather than nihilism and paranoid conceptions of individual aggrandizement that should promote a healthy professional culture.

Contents of discursive practice are partially based on Foucaultean thought which views a corpus of knowledge in its continuity—in an historico-transcendental schemata—as a system of dispersion (Foucault, 1972). Discursive discourse is a radically dynamic style and method; it views—as I would like to interpret—a homeless person as an independent autonomous person who is somehow disconnected with his mundane possessions. Many people, by the same logic, are poor not because of their pathologies—as the predominant doctrines would have us believe—but due to systemic linkages which reward acquisitiveness against nonpossesiveness. The role of knowledge is to explain these power polarities. Discursive dialogue employs an empowering vocabulary: there are people, not clients; situations, not problems; and transformation, not therapy.

It is an attempt to reveal discursive practices in their complexity and density; to show that to speak is to do something—something other than to express what one thinks; to translate what one knows, and something other than to play with the structures of language (*langue*); to show that to add a statement to a pre-existing series of statements is to perform a complicated and costly gesture, which involves conditions . . . and rules; to show that a change in the order of discourse does not presuppose "new ideas," a little invention and creativity, a different mentality, but transformations in a practice, perhaps also in neighboring practices, and in their common articulation. (Foucault, 1972: 209)

Michel Foucault conceives of discursive formulations, positivitites, and knowledge in the context of the episteme which "is the totality of relations that can be discovered, for a given period, between the sciences when one analyzes them at the level of discursive regularities" (Foucault, 1972: 191). Afro-American alienation in the present day conditions, for example, may be better understood if the history, economics, and politics of slavery are studied in the continuity of human oppression. Likewise, the revolt of Dalits in contemporary India calls for demystification of the mythology that has institutionalized inequality along caste lines without any possibility of change (Desai, Monteiro, and Narayan, 1998: 59, 1). Discursive analysis, it can be argued, is a viable means of legitimizing social transformation on the basis of historical knowledge. The readers can apply this mode of analysis to any problematic situation. Answers revealed will be different than offered by traditional practitioners.

In sum, an argument may be offered to deconstruct the whole epistemology of contemporary social world. People, in the contexts of their problems and possibilities, ought to be studied as a new continuity despite their discontinuities. In closing, Foucault says it best:

To reveal in all its purity the space in which discursive events are deployed is not to undertake to re-establish it in an isolation that nothing could overcome; it is not to close it upon itself; it is to leave oneself free to describe the interplay of relations within it and outside it. (Foucault, 1972: 29)

Before Edward Wilson wrote *Consilience* (1998) and Eileen Gambrill talked about "critical thinking" (1997), this author critically unraveled the human condition and called for the unification of science and arts, facts and values toward a holistic understanding of the developmental processes that cause human oppression (Mohan, 1987: 85–96; 1992; 1993; 1996). Discontinuities and thresholds mark the future of continuity. The millennial rupture is equally fraught with discontinuities and positivities; hope and nihilism; and the known and unknown. Social work as we knew it in the twentieth century is bound to evolve into a new identity rather than dissolve in the conceptual anomalies of an ossified past. Y2K—the glitch, after all, turned out to be a management problem!

As I invent Being starting from Being, and return to Being on the surface of Being, I am exactly in the situation of the creator. (Sartre, 1992: 29)

NOTE

The author acknowledges gratitude and deep appreciation to the Tata Institute of Social Sciences, Mumbi, India, for permission to use the concluding article of a Special Issue of their Indian *Journal of Social Work*, January 1999 (Mohan, 1999).

Epilogue: A Fulcrum of Inanity

I do not think that subsequent American leftists have made any advance on Dewey's understudying of the relation between the individual and society. Dewey was as convinced as Foucault that the subject is a social construction, that discursive practices go all the way down to the bottom of our minds and hearts. But he insisted that the only point of society is to construct subjects capable of ever more novel, ever richer, forms of human happiness. The vocabulary in which Dewey suggested we discuss our social problems and our political initiatives was part of his attempt to develop a discursive practice suitable for that project of social reconstruction.

—Richard Rorty (1998: 31)

By accepting vocabularies of misguided change, social scientists developed a neurotic urge to blame rather than feel responsible. This lack of good faith eventually culminated into a dysfunctional culture where intervention, rather than reconstruction—therapy rather than dialogue—became the heart of professional culture. Scientific theories and laws of nature only reinforced a cult of objectivity and we all became disciples of a self-infatuated discipline.

As social work celebrates its 100th anniversary, a summit is held "to unify the profession's voice" on main issues.[1] "The future of social programs that help the nation's poor and employ social workers depends on whether American women organize to harness their huge political potential," Richard Cloward told the Social Work Summit participants (NASW, 1998: 1). In other words, we social workers depend on poor people for our existence. We also depend on women's organizations: "The attack on the welfare state is an attack on women and our jobs. . . . The future of the welfare state depends on women winning that war," Cloward contended. Women's development as a political force is "our only hope," he said (NASW, 1998: 6). It seems that welfare state, as an institution by itself, is not an issue. Also, neither poverty nor its feminization is our main concern. We are primarily concerned about their political clout which can generate certain social programs that offer job opportunities. Poverty and inequality, obviously, are not our concerns. This explains the problem of social work.

There is a conspicuous lack of unison discussion about central issues. Perhaps it is incompatible with the logic of a hyper democracy. A fragmented, often adhocist, minimalist approach seems to please ever one. We play games. Game theory becomes a rationale for compromises. Incremental changes and piecemeal solutions substitute when we need an overhaul. Our self-congratulatory chapters in the formidable volumes of encyclopedias become obsolete by the time they reach the readers. Careerism, territoriality, and self-infatuation have generated a counterculture that promotes mediocrity, premature complacence and interest-constitutive growth at the expense of progress, development, and civility.

Diversity, which should be our strength, has become a source of territorial-dysfunctionality. The outcome is a massive alienation of people from the theory and practice of their calling. A pervasive sense of inanity—irrelevance, impudence, and ineffectiveness—pervades introspective analysis. Norman Levitt, professor of mathematics at Rutgers University, has a point: "The relationship of the intellectual left to the day-to-day politics of the surrounding society has decayed to the point of non-existence," he writes. "Forces of economic and social change work themselves out in ways that these thinkers can hardly apprehend, let alone influence."[2]

Leo Tolstoy in *My Confession* talks about "four means of escape from the terrible state in which we all were": ignorance, Epicureanism, suicide, and acquiescence (Tolstoy, 1995: 35–39). He wrote:

Thus do those of my own class, in four different ways, save themselves from a terrible contradiction. With the most earnest intellectual efforts I could not find a fifth way. One way is to ignore life's being a meaningless jumble of vanity and evil—not to know that it is better not to live. For me not to know this was impossible; and when I saw truth, I could not shut my eyes to it. Another way is to make the best of life as it is without thinking of the future. This, again, I could not do.... The third way is, knowing that life is an evil and a foolish thing, to put an end to it, to kill one's self. I understood this, but still did not kill myself. The fourth way is to accept life as described by Solomon and Schopenhauer, to know that it is stupid and ridiculous joke, and yet live on, to wash, dress, dine, talk, and even write books. This position was painful and disgusting to me, but I remained in it. (Tolstoy, 1995: 37–38)

It seems to me that most introspective social workers, despite angelic hearts, commit themselves to the fourth escape in a gamut of roles without substantially changing the oppressive structures of dogma and/or design. Inability to change the system is not necessarily one's weakness; to do nothing, however, is a sign of intellectual cowardice.

As a fulcrum of inanity, social work has come to epitomize the failure of science in general, social sciences in particular. Social transformation, a goal enshrined in the spirit of Enlightenment, calls for: (1) new vocabularies of change, (2) innovative means of transmutation, and (3) a progressive discourse that redefines the genius of a dynamic culture. Having achieved these attributes, one would hope for a future that will embrace both peace and justice for all. The present, guided by its past, is always a preparatory ground for the new and challenging directions.

NASW's Code of Ethics is a noble and liberating document. It reflects the vision and hope of a professional community that is engaged in constructive projects. Yet, one cannot say that our loftier ethical goals and standards always serve as our guides and we are anywhere close to solving our problems. In other words, a hiatus—representing our dilemmas—continues to plague our progress. This paradox remains a formidable obstacle to achieving our avowed objectives. A profession that thrives on cultural narcissism cannot be a vehicle of any meaningful social change. Consummate professionals have to go beyond atavistic careerism. At every level, in every sphere, a shocking chasm of redundancy and reform constitutes the anatomy of a failure of ideology and practice. This schizophrenic dualism of our public policy, social research, and social practice warrants a new approach to overcome the inanity of intervention.

The "diversity" of social work theory masquerades as an eclectic medium of "interlocking" more than twenty theoretical systems (Turner, 1997: 2258–2265; 1986). Since "social work is socially constructed through interactions with clients, its 'theory'," contends Malcolm Payne, "at any time is constructed by the same social forces that construct the activity" (Payne, 1997: 24–25). Payne's "social construction view" is premised on agreed upon "understandings within various social grouping" which implies "a struggle between competing understandings and construction.... That struggle is a politics" (Payne, 1997: 25). The politics of diversity, it may be added, has dearly cost an otherwise benign eclecticism. A mindless application of borrowed constructs without any reciprocal interaction amounts to a one-way traffic which breeds academic parasitism at best. Furthermore, this expedience of unilateral exchange, which generally involves a "cut-and-paste" approach, can hardly lead to authenticity let alone enduring legitimation. When struggle is political, everything-goes attitude perverts both the mission and the methodology. It's about time to deconstruct the diversity discourse.

In the Age of Enlightenment, knowledge—put simply—replaced politics. However, positivists' politics of objectivity led to a new dogmatic rationality separating facts and values. Not until interpretivist, deconstructivist, and hermeneutics altered emphases and redefined social reality, perspectives on human affairs became clearer, and multi-dimensional. Social work's legacy of functionalist-positivist past continues to obscure the new reality: empancipatory praxis. A new Enlightenment warrants Social Contract II as the new millennium imperative. Epiphanies of discordant voices have produced a balkanizing chorus dividing the soul of the substance, ethic, and mandate.

In his last book, *The Conflict of Faculties*, Immanuel Kant attempted to divorce philosophy from politics (Kant, [1979] 1992). Foucaultian revolt against Kant's view seeks a remarriage of knowledge and power. If knowledge is power, specialized scientific disciplines assume hierarchical character of power. These islands of knowledge, despite interdisciplinarity, remain fragmented engines in the knowledge production industry that manufactures recipes of inequality and injustice. Postindustrial universities and other centers of specialized disciplines are new feudal domains in the entrepreneurial jungle. One successful Bill Gates leaves behind millions of failures. Organizational hierarchies of specialized knowledge have created a new caste system which anoints and relegates differential roles and statuses in accordance with its own interests. To expect equality and fairness in a field where laws of new barbarianism prevail may be called idiocy of the learned. The present legitimation crisis, fundamentally, is a struggle against the pervasive devolution of knowledge.

The knowledge devolution has transformed the institutional culture where new specializations develop and grow. The new ethic of privatization has delegitimized every value and structure that concerned public welfare. In a marketplace where fund-raising has become the ultimate goal, development and research play the politics of euphemism. Academia, which ought to be the temple of truth, has become an arena of vested interests where the clout of the privilege, rather than the weight of individual merit, determines one's worth. Arbitrarily designed and imposed definitions of merit have short-changed virtues and pampered spurious scholarship. The demise of dissent is a manifestation of the power of an invisible third force that symbolizes the rise of an institutional McCarthyism that is corrupting the temples of knowledge.

Social work remains epistemologically challenged in varied fields and endeavors of professional import. Our intellectual parasitism does not absolve us of our moral obligations. Interdiciplinarity is not a one-way traffic. If we cannot repay our debts, we remain terminally bankrupt. I have seldom seen social work formulations and "theories" adopted, utilized, and critiqued by other cognate disciplines. Our journals, by and large, represent the kitsch of contemporary productivity. *Zeitgeist* of social work is a fictional reality in the minds of those whose territorial instincts legitimize an unjust universe. "The story of social work as virtue, as helping and empowerment, may be familiar," but critically, as argued by Leslie Margolin, "it is neither 'natural' nor obvious" (Margolin, 1997: xiii). Margolin questions, "whether we can peer behind the familiar images to locate meanings more ironic than lofty, where self-interest poses as knowledge, and knowledge is an instrument of power . . . consider how social work's mild-mannered eclecticism maybe the most presumptuous ideology of all since it pretends to have no ideology" (Margolin, 1997: xiii).

What can we do to improve the state of knowledge? Much of it lies in the dispassionate analysis and context of sociology of social work: people with whom we work, problems that we attempt to resolve; organizational contexts that circumscribe our tools; methods that we employ; theories that we formulate; practices that we adopt; and ideologies that we profess and practice. I intend to explore some of these dimensions and issues in a sequel to this work (Mohan, forthcoming). In the meanwhile, I suggest we ought to read and revise our fundamental understanding of the democratic processes that humanize education. John Dewey's biographer Robert Westbrook argues:

Among liberal intellectuals of the twentieth century, Dewey was the most important advocate of participatory democracy, that is, of the belief that democracy as an ethical ideal calls upon men and women to build communities in which the necessaries opportunities and resources are available for every individual to realize fully his or her particular capacities and powers through participation in political, social, and cultural life. This ideal rested on a "faith in the capacity of human beings for intelligent judgement and action if proper conditions are furnished," a faith, Dewey argued, *so deeply embedded in the methods which are intrinsic to democracy that when a professed democrat denies the faith he convicts himself of treachery to his profession*". (Westbrook, 1991: xiv–xv in Kaplan and Levine, 1997: 56–57; emphasis added)

NOTES

1. The Social Work Summit held in Washington, D.C., among leaders of more than 40 organizations was "a major step toward a unified profession with a single, powerful voice," Josephine Allen, President, National Association of Social Workers reported (NASW, 1998: 1).

2. "Skeptic Magazine" (Autumn 1998): http://www.skeptic.com/magazine.html (*The Chronicle's World-Wide Web*, November 23, 1998).

Bibliography

Adler, Jerry. 1977. "Unbeliever's Quest." *Newsweek*, March 31: 64–65.

Advocate. 1996. "The Evolution of Child Care" (cartoon). Baton Rouge, LA, August 27: 6B.

———. 1995. Baton Rouge, LA, January 15: 8B.

———. 1994. *Associated Press* story. Baton Rouge, LA, June 2: 14A.

Agrest, Susan. 1997. "Kids Who Care." *Time*, December 15: 132–134.

Apel, Karl-Otto. 1984. *Understanding and Explanation: A Transcendental-Pragmatic Perspective*. trans. G. Warnke. Cambridge, MA: MIT Press.

———. [1972] 1980. *Toward a Transformation of Philosophy*. trans. G. Adey and D. Frisby. London: Routledge & Kegan Paul.

Appleyard, Brian. 1993. *Understanding the Present: Science and the Soul of Modern Man*. New York: Doubleday.

Arendt, Hannah. [1948] 1979. *The Origins of Totalitarianism*. New York: Harcourt Brace.

Armey, Dick. 1995. *Revolution: A Strategy for the Rebirth of Freedom*. Washington, D.C.: Eagle Publishing Co.

Associated Press. 1996. "Congressional Honor Given to Graham." Baton Rouge, LA: *Advocate*, 3A.

———. 1995. February 3.

———. 1995a. June 29.

———. 1994. June 19.

Austin, David. 1997. "The Profession of Social Work in the Second Century," in Michael Reich and Eileen Gambrill (1997: 396–407).

Baird, Vanessa. 1994. "Spiked" (Media Keynote). *New Internationalist*, 256, June: 4–7.

Barlett, Donald L. and James B. Steele. 1998. "Corporate Welfare." *Time*, November 9: 36–39.

Becker, Ernest. 1975. *Escape from Evil*. New York: Free Press.

———. 1974. "The Discovery of the Science of Man," in John M. Romanyshan (1974, 7–32).

———. 1968. *The Structure of Evil: An Essay on the Unification of the Science of Man*. New York: The Free Press.

Bell, Daniel. 1960. *The End of Ideology: On the Exhaustion of Political Ideas in the Fifties*. Glencoe, IL: Free Press.

Bellafante, Gina. 1998. "Feminism: It's All about Me." *Time*, June 29: 54–62.

Bellah, Robert N., R. Madsen, William M. Sullivan, et al. 1985. *Habits of the Heart: Individualism and Commitment in American Life*. New York: Harper & Row.

Berger, Peter L. and Thomas Luckmann. 1966. *The Social Construction of Reality: A Treatise in the Sociology of Knowledge*. Garden City, NY: Doubleday & Co.

Bernstein, Richard J., ed. 1985. *Habermas and Modernity*. Cambridge, MA: MIT Press.

Bhaumik, Subir, Meenakshi Ganguly, and Tim McGirk. 1997. "Seeker of Souls." *Time*, September 15: 78–84.

Birnbaum, Norman. 1988. *The Radical Renewal: The Politics of Ideas in Modern America*. New York: Pantheon Books.

Blackburn, Robin. 1998. "The Irrepressible Left." *Dissent*, Fall: 42–46.

Brecher, Jeremy and Tim Costello. 1994. *Global Village or Global Pillage?* Boston: South End Press.

Broder, David. 1995. "Our Best Hopes Lie in Two Words," Washington Post Writers' Group. Baton Rouge, LA: *Sunday Advocate*, January 1: 12B.

———. 1995a. "Dole Should Extend Criticism," Washington Post Writers' Group. Baton Rouge, LA: *Sunday Advocate*, 10B.

———. 1995b. "No Doubt about Dick Armey's Philosophy," Washington Post Writers' Group. Baton Rouge, LA: *Advocate*, June 21: 9B.

———. 1994. "Soaring Illegitimacy Must Be Curtailed," Washington Post Writers' Group. Baton Rouge, LA: *Advocate*, June 22: 7B.

Brown, Norman O. 1959. *The Psychoanalytic Meaning of History*. New York: Viking.

Camus, Albert. 1986. *Neither Victims, nor Executioners*, trans. D. MacDonald. Philadelphia, PA: New Society Publishers.

Carbonnier, Gilles. 1998. *Conflict, Postwar Rebuilding and the Economy: A Critical Review of the Literature*. War-torn Societies Project Occasional Paper No. 2, Geneva: UNRISD.

Chiari, Joseph. 1975. *Twentieth Century French Thought: From Bergson to Levi-Strauss*. New York: Gordian Press.

Ciabattari, Jane. 1997. "Five Teens Who Are Changing the World." *Parade Magazine*, April 27: 19.

Cloud, John. 1998. "Why Coors Went Soft." *Time*, November 2: 70.

Collins, Randall. 1994. *Four Sociological Traditions*. New York: Oxford University Press.

———, ed. 1994a. *Four Sociological Traditions: Selected Readings*. New York: Oxford University Press.

Coupland, Douglas. 1991. *Generation X: Tales of Accelerated Culture*. New York: St. Martin's Press.

Craib, Ian. 1985. *Modern Social Theory: From Parsons to Habermas*. Brighton, Sussex: Wheatsheaf.

Crary, David. 1995. "Nuclear Plan Draws Outrage," Associated Press. Baton Rouge, LA: *Advocate*, June 15: 13A.

Crews, Frederick. 1993. "The Unknown Freud," *The New York Review of Books*, XL, 19: 55–65.

Dasgupta, Partha. 1995. *An Inquiry Into Well-Being and Destitution*. New York: Oxford University Press.

Dejean, Joan. 1997. *Ancients Against Moderns: Culture Wars and the Making of a Fin de Siècle*. Chicago: University of Chicago.

de Madariaga, Salvador. 1946. *Victors Beware*. London: Jonathan Cape.

Derrida, Jacques. 1994. *Spectres of Marx: The State of the Debt, the Work of Mourning, and the New International*, trans. Peggy Kamuff. London: Routledge.

———. 1991. *A Derrida Reader: Between the Blinds*. New York: Columbia University Press.

Desai, M., A. Monteiro, and L. Narayan, eds. 1998. "Toward People-Centered Development," *The Indian Journal of Social Work*, Special Issue, 59, 1: 1–2.

Diesing, Paul. 1991. *How Does Social Science Work? Reflections on Practice*. Pittsburgh, PA: University of Pittsburgh Press.

Dixon, John and Robert P. Scheurell, eds. 1995. *Social Welfare with Indigenous Peoples*. London: Routledge.

Dolgov, Anna. 1998. "Russia Dealing with Grass-Root Anti-Semitism." Baton Rouge, LA: *Advocate*, November 13: 12A.

Douston, Diane. 1996. "Working Poor's Children a Third on Poverty Rolls," Associated Press. Baton Rouge, LA: *Advocate*, June 3: 1A.

Ehrenreich, Barbara. 1983. *The Hearts of Men: American Dreams and the Flight From Commitment*. Garden City, NY: Anchor.

Elmer-Dewitt, Phillip. 1995. "Cyberporn," *Time*, July 3: 38–45.

Engelhardt, Tom. 1995. *The End of Victory Culture*. New York: Basic Books.

Epstein, William M. 1997. *Welfare in America: How Social Science Fails the Poor*. Madison: University of Wisconsin Press.

———. 1995. Letter to the Editor, *Journal of Social Work Education*, 31: 132–33.

———. 1994. "Economic Development and Social Welfare in the Third World," *Journal of International & Comparative Social Welfare*, X, 2: 107–136.

———. 1993. *The Dilemma of American Social Welfare*. New Brunswick: Transaction Publishers.

Faludi, Susan, 1991. *Backlash: The Undeclared War against American Women*. New York: Crown.

Ferris, Timothy. 1993. "The Case against Science," *The New York Review of Books*, XL, 9, May 13: 17–19.

Feyerabend, Paul. [1975] 1988. *Against Method*. London: Verso.

———. 1978. *Science in a Free Society*. London: New Left Books.

Fischer, Joel. 1981. "The Social Work Revolution," *Social Work*, 26, 3: 199–207.

———. 1973. "Is Casework Effective: A Review." *Social Work*, 18, 4: 5–20.

Fish, S. 1990. *Doing What Comes Naturally: Change, Rhetoric, and the Practice of Theory in Library and Legal Studies*. Durham, NC: Duke University Press.

Flexner, A. 1915. "Is Social Work a Profession?" in *Proceedings of the National Conference of Charities and Correction*. Chicago: Hildman Printing, 576–590.

Foucault, Michel. [1972] 1993. *The Archaeology of Knowledge & the Discourse on Language*, trans. A. M. Sheridan Smith. New York: Barnes & Noble.

Fromm, Erich. 1957. "Man Is Not a Thing." *Saturday Review*, March 16: 9–11.

———. 1947. *Man for Himself: An Inquiry into the Psychology of Ethics*. New York: Rinehart & Co.

———. 1941. *Escape from Freedom*. New York: Farrar and Rinehart.

Fuchs, Stephan. 1992. *The Professional Quest for Truth: A Social Theory of Science and Knowledge*. New York: State University of New York Press.

Fukuyama, Francis. 1989. "The End of History," *National Interest*: 3–19.

Gambrill, E. 1997. *Social Work Practice: A Critical Thinker's Guide*. New York: Oxford University Press.

Gehlen, Arnold. 1963. "Uber kulturelle Kristallisation," *Studien zur Anthropologie*. Neuwied: 321.

Geismar, L. L. 1982. "Debate with Authors: Comments on the Scientific Imperative in Social Work Research." *Social Service Review*, 56, 2: 311–312.

Gelernter, David. 1997. *Drawing Life: Surviving the Unabomber*. New York:

Free Press (excerpted in *Time*, "How I Survived the Unabomber," September 22: 82–90).

Gibbs, Nancy. 1996. "Cause Celeb," *Time*, June 17: 28–30.

———. 1995. "Working Harder, Getting No Where," *Time*, July 3: 16–20.

———. 1994. "The Vicious Cycle," *Time*, June 20: 24–33.

Gil, David G. 1990. *Unraveling Social Policy*. Rochester, VT: Schenkman Books.

Goodman, Ellen. 1995. "Technology Is Fast, but Understanding Takes Time," Washington Post Writer's Group. Baton Rouge, LA: *Advocate*, June 16: 7B.

Gordon, William E. 1983. "Social Work Revolution or Evolution?" *Social Work*, 28, 3, 181–185.

Gore, Al. 1992. *Earth in the Balance*. New York: Houghton Miffin Co.

Gould, Stephen J. 1998. *Questioning the Millennium: A Rationalist's Guide to a Precise Arbitrary Countdown*. New York: Harmony Books.

Gourevitch, Phillip. 1996. "Misfortune Tellers: In a New Trend, Hell Is Other Peoples." *The New Yorker*, April 6: 96–100.

Graff, James L. 1996. "The Gorilla of America's Dreams," *Time*, September 2: 70.

Gramsci, Antonio. [1957] 1992. *The Modern Prince & Other Writings*. New York: International Publishers.

Grene, Marjorie. 1973. *Sartre*. New York: New Viewpoints.

Grinnell, Richard M., Carol D. Austin, and Betty J. Blythe, et al. 1994. "Social Work Researchers' Quest for Respectability," *Social Work*, 39, 4: 469–470.

Gross, Paul R. and Norman Levitt. 1994. *Higher Superstition: The Academic Left and Its Quarrels with Science*. Baltimore, MD: Johns Hopkins University Press.

Grunbaum, Adolf. 1984. *The Foundations of Psychoanalysis*. Berkeley: University of California Press.

Habermas, Jurgen. 1989. "Twenty Years Later: 1968 & the West German Republic." *Dissent*, Spring, 252.

———. 1987. *The Philosophical Discourse on Modernity: Twelve Lectures*. trans. Frederick Lawrence, Cambridge, MA: The MIT Press.

———. 1987a. *The Theory of Communicative Action: Lifeword and Systems: A Critique of the Functionalist Reason*. trans. T. McCarthy. Boston: Beacon Press.

———. 1984. *The Theory of Communicative Action: Reason and the Rationalization of Society*. trans. T. McMarthy. Boston: Beacon Press.

———. 1981. "Modernity Versus Postmodernity," *New German Critique*, Winter: 22.

———. 1975. *Legitimacy Crisis*. trans. T. McCarthy. Boston: Beacon Press.

———. 1974. *Theory and Practice*. trans. J. Viertal. London: Heinemann.

————. 1972. *Knowledge and Human Interest*. trans. J. J. Shapiro. London: Heinemann.

————. [1970] 1988. *On the Logic of Social Science*. Cambridge, MA: MIT Press.

Hacker, Andrew. 1992. *Two Nations*. New York: Scribner's.

Halpert, Julie E. 1996. "Harnessing the Sun and Selling It Abroad: U.S. Solar Industry in Export Boom." *The New York Times*, June 5: C1.

Handleman, Stephen. 1995. *Comrade Criminal: The New Russian Mafia*. New Haven, CT: Yale University Press.

Hanley, Charles J. 1996. "Human Now Urban Species: 'City summit' Facing Huge Challenge." Baton Rouge, LA: *Sunday Advocate*, May 26: 12B.

Hardwick, E. ed. 1963. *Letters of William James*. New York: Anchor Books.

Hasan, S. Z. 1995. Personal communication.

Havel, Vaclav. 1998. "The Charms of NATO," *The New York Review of Books*, January 15: XLV, 1:24.

————. 1995. "The Responsibility of Intellectuals," *The New York Review of Books*, XLII (11), June 22: 36–37.

————. 1994. "What the World Needs Now," *New Age Journal*, October, 45–46; 161–162.

————. 1991. *Disturbing the Peace*. New York: Vintage Books.

Haworth, Glenn O. 1991. "My Paradigm Can Beat Your Paradigm: Some Reflection on Knowledge Conflicts." *Journal of Sociology & Social Welfare*, 35–49.

Heineman, Martha B. 1981. "The Obsolete Scientific Imperative in Social Work Research." *Social Service Review*, 55, 3: 371–396.

Held, D., J. Anderson, and B. Gieben, et al., eds. 1983. *States and Societies*. New York: New York University Press.

Hentoff, Nat. 1996. "Journalist Carrying on Fight against Slavery." Baton Rouge, LA: *Advocate*, June 18: 7B.

Herrnstein, R. and C. Murray, 1994. *The Bell Curve*. New York: The Free Press.

Hopps, June G. 1994. *U.S. News & World Report*, March 21: 97.

Hobsbawm, Eric. 1995. *The Age of Extremes: A History of the World. 1914–1991*. New York: Pantheon.

Hornblower, Margot. 1997. "Great eXpectation," *Time*, June 9: 58–69.

Horowitz, A. and T. Maley. 1994. *Barbarism of Reason*. Toronto: University of Toronto Press.

Howe, David. 1987. *An Introduction to Social Work Theory*. Brookfield, VT: Wildwood House.

Hughes, Candice. 1994. "Organized Crime Mugging Russian Economy," *Associated Press*. Baton Rouge, LA: *Advocate*, June 1: 8A.

Huntington, Samuel P. 1996. "The West: Unique, Not Universal." *Foreign Affairs*, November/December, 75, 6: 28–46.

Isaacson, Walter. 1997–1998. "Man of the Year . . . Driven by the Passion of Intel's." *Time*, December 29–January 5: 48–51.

Jay, Martin. 1985. "Habermas and Modernism," in Richard J. Bernstein (1985: 125–139).

Jones, Lisa. 1994. *Bulletproof Lisa: Tales of Race, Sex, and Hair*. New York: Doubleday.

Judt, T. 1995. "Downhill All the Way," *The New York Review of Books*, XLII (9) May 25: 20–25.

Kant, Immanuel. [1979] 1992. *Conflict of Faculties*. trans. Mary J. Gregor. Lincoln: University of Nebraska Press.

———. 1958. *Critique of Pure Reason*. trans. Norman, Kemp, Smith. London: Macmillan.

Kaplan, E. Ann and George Levine, eds. 1997. *The Politics of Research*. New Brunswick, NJ: Rutgers University Press.

Kaplan, L. 1992. "Antimetaphysics and the Liberal Quandary," *Philosophy of Social Sciences*, 22, 4 (December): 492–511.

Katz, Stanley N. 1997. "The Scholar-Teacher, the University and Society." in Kaplan and Levine (1997: 46–58).

Kaus, Mickey. 1992. *The End of Equality*. New York: Basic Books.

Keat, Russell. 1981. *The Politics of Social Theory*. Chicago, IL: The University of Chicago Press.

Keeley, Lawrence. 1996. *War Before Civilization*. New York: Oxford.

Kerman, Alvin, ed. 1997. *What's Happened to the Humanities?* New Jersey: Princeton.

Khinduka, Shanti K. 1965. "The Meaning of Social Work," in S. K. Khinduka, ed., *Social Work in India*. Allahabad: Kitab Mahal.

Kierkegaard, Soren. [1849] 1941. *The Sickness Unto Death*. trans. Walter Laurie. Princeton, NJ: Princeton University Press.

Kohut, Heinz. 1971. *The Analysis of the Self: A Systematic Approach to the Psychoanalytic Treatment of Narcissistic Personality Disorder*. New York: International University Press.

Kondracke, Morton. 1998. "Public Likes President's Policy." Baton Rouge, LA: Advocate January 6: 7B.

Kramer, Michael. 1996. "Russia '96: People Choose." *Time*, May 27: 49–57.

———. 1995. "The Poverty of Compassion," *Time*, January 16: 32.

Kreuger, Larry W. 1997. "The End of Social Work," *Journal of Social Work Education*, 33, 1: 19–27.

Kuhn, Thomas S. [1962] 1996. *The Structure of Scientific Revolutions*. Chicago, IL: University of Chicago Press.

Kulig, Magda. 1995. "Walesa Silent on Anti-Semitic Sermon," Associated Press. Baton Rouge, LA: *Sunday Advocate*, June 18: 12A.

Laing, R. D. 1967. *The Politics of Experience*. New York: Ballantine Books.

Lasch, Christopher. 1978. *The Culture of Narcissism: American Life in an Age of Diminishing Expectations*. New York: Norton.

Lenhardt, Christian K. 1972. "Rise and Fall of Transcendental Anthropology," *Philosophy of the Social Sciences*, 2: 231–246.

Lewontin, Richard C. 1998. "Survival of the Nicest?" *The New York Review of Books*, October 22, XLV, 16: 59–63.

Lind, Michael. 1995. "American by Invitation," *The New Yorker*, April 24: 107–113.

———. 1995a. *The Next American Nation: The New Nationalism and the Fourth American Revolution*. New York: The Free Press.

———. 1994. *The Next American Nation: The Origins and Future of American Identity*. New York: The Free Press.

Lindley, David. 1993. *The End of Physics: The Myth of a Unified Theory*. New York: Basic Books.

Lobkowicz, Nikolaus, F. R. Dallmayr, C. K. Lenhardt, M. A. Hill, and C. Nichols. 1972. "Review Symposium on Habermas," *Philosophy of Social Science*, 2: 193–270.

Lucas, Christopher J. 1996. *Crisis in the Academy: Rethinking Higher Education in America*. New York: St. Martin's.

Macmillan, Malcolm. 1991. *Freud, Evaluated: The Complete Arc*. New York: North-Holland.

Marcuse, Herbert. 1970. *Five Lectures: Psychoanalysis, Politics, and Utopia*. trans. Jeremy J. Shapiro and Shierry M. Weber. Boston: Beacon.

———. [1941] 1968. *Reason and Revolution: Hegel and the Rise of Social Theory*. Boston: Beacon.

———. 1964. *One-Dimensional Man: Studies in the Ideology of Advanced Industrial Society*. Boston: Beacon.

———. 1955. *Eros and Civilization: A Philosophical Inquiry into Freud*. Boston: Beacon.

Margoline, Leslie. 1997. *Under the Cover of Kindness: The Invention of Social Work*. Charlottsville, VA: University Press of Georgia.

Marquardt, Manfred. 1992. *John Wiley's Social Ethics: Praxis and Principles*, trans. John E. Steely & W. Stephen Gunter. Nashville: Abingdon Press.

Mills, C. Wright. 1959. *The Sociological Imagination*. New York: Oxford University Press.

———. 1956. *The Elite Power*. New York: Oxford University Press.

Mishra, Ramesh. 1984. *The Welfare State in Crisis*. New York: St Martin's.

Mohan, B. forthcoming. *The Other Profession: Sociology of Social Work*.

———. 1999. "Social Work: The End or a New Beginning?" *Indian Journal of Social Work* (Special Issue), co-eds. Kenneth I. Millar and B. Mohan. January, 60, 1: 168–181.

———. 1997. A letter in *Time*, September 15: 18.

———. 1997a. "Toward New Global Development," *International Social Work*, 40, 4: 433–450.

———. 1997b. "The Professional Quest for Truth: Paradigm, Paradox, and Praxis." *International Journal of Contemporary Sociology*. 34, 1: 51–63.

———. 1996. *Democracies of Unfreedom: The United States of America and India*. Westport, CT: Praeger.

———. 1996a. "Self, Society, and Science: On Transforming Social Reality." *International Journal of Contemporary Sociology*, 33, 1: 59–78.

———. 1996b. "Against De-development: Toward a New Social Work," Paper delivered to the Joint World Congress of the International Federation of Social Workers and the International Association of Schools of Social Work 1996 on Participating in Change: The Social Work Profession in Social Development, Hong Kong, July 24–27 (*Proceedings*, 121–124); also in *New Global Development: Journal of International and Comparative Social Welfare*, 1996, XII: 99–105.

———. 1995. "Reinventing the Mission." *New Global Development: Journal of International and Comparative Social Welfare*, XI: 74–78.

———. 1993. *Eclipse of Freedom: The World of Oppression*. Westport, CT: Praeger.

———. 1993a. "Diversity and Conflict: Toward a Unified Model of Social Work," *Indian Journal of Social Work*, LIV, 4: 597–608.

———. 1992. *Global Development: Post-Material Values and Social Praxis*. New York: Praeger.

———. 1988. *The Logic of Social Welfare: Conjectures and Formulations*. New York: St. Martin's.

———. 1987. *Denial of Existence: Essays on the Human Condition*. Springfield, IL: Charles C. Thomas.

———. ed. 1985. *New Horizons in Social Welfare and Policy*. Cambridge, MA: Schenkman.

———. ed. 1985a. *Toward Comparative Social Welfare*. Cambridge, MA: Schenkman.

———. 1980. "Human Behavior, Social Environment, Social Reconstruction, and Social Policy: A System of Linkage, Goals, and Priorities," *Journal of Education for Social Work*, 16, 2: 26–32.

———. 1972. *Social Psychiatry in India: A Treatise on the Mentally Ill*. Calcutta: Minerva.

———. 1972a. "Prison Problems in India," *International Journal of Offender Therapy & Comparative Criminology*, XVI, 1: 32–34.

———. 1971. "An Indian Study of Prison Psychosis," *International Journal of Offender Therapy*, XV, 3: 207–314.

———. 1963. "Social Work and the Problem of Mental Disorders: A Study of Selected Cases of Mental Disorders Hospitalized in the Mental Hospitals of Agra, Bareilly, and Varanasi and in the Districts of Agra,

Aligarh, and Mathura." Luckonw: Lucknow University, Doctoral Dissertation.

Moore, Thomas. 1965. *Utopia*. London: Penguin Books.

Morales, Armando T. and Bradford W. Sheafor. [1977] 1992. *Social Work: A Profession of Many Faces*. Boston: Allyn and Bacon.

Morrow, Lance. 1994–1995. "Yin and Yang, Sleaze and Moralizing," *Time*, December 16/January 2: 158.

National Association of Social Workers (NASW). 1998. "Summit's Aim: Profession's Unity," *NASWNEWS*. Washington, D.C.: NASW, November, 43, 10: 1–2.

Naylor, Robert, Jr. 1994. "Haves and Havenots in U.S. Work Force Face Widening Gap." Baton Rouge, LA: *Advocate*, June 3: 1A.

New York Review of Books. 1995. "Rethinking Social Development: An International Conference," XLII, (4), March 2: 29.

Nietzsche, Friedrich W. 1966. *Beyond Good and Evil*. trans. Walter Kaufmann. New York: Vintage Books.

———. 1956. *The Genealogy of Morals*. trans. Francis Golffing. Garden City, NJ: Doubleday & Co.

Office of Independent Council. 1998. *Referral to the United States House of Representatives pursuant to Title 28, United States Code, §595(c)* (September 9).

Ohmae, Kenichi. 1995. *The End of the Nation State*. New York: The Free Press.

Ortega y Gasset, Jose. [1932] 1957. *The Revolt of the Masses*. New York: W. W. Norton.

Overby, Dennis. 1993. "Who Is Afraid of the Big Band Bang?" *Time*, April 26: 74.

Page, Clarence. 1995. "If Affirmative Action Isn't Dead, It's Weakened," Tribune Media Service. Baton Rouge, LA: *Advocate*, June 20: 7B.

Parade Magazine. 1995. "UN Responds to Fears," June 25: 15.

Parsons, Talcott. 1951. *The Social System*. New York: The Free Press.

Payne, Malcolm. 1997. *Modern Social Work Theory*. Chicago: Lyceum.

Peck, Grant. 1995. "Cyberspace Activists Enjoy Free Rein, World Stage," Associated Press. Baton Rouge, LA: *Advocate*, April 23: 19A.

Phillips, Kevin. 1994. *Arrogant Capital: Washington, Wall Street and the Frustration of American Politics*. New York: Little, Brown.

Pipes, Richard. 1994. *Communism: The Vanished Specter*. Oslo: Scandinavian University Press.

Quinn, Daniel. 1993. *Ishmael: An Adventure of the Mind and Spirit*. New York: Bantam/Turner.

Quinn-Judge, Paul. 1997. "Wolves on the Prowl." *Time*, December 15: 58.

Raspberry, William. 1995. "Are We There Yet with Affirmative Action?"

Washington Post Writers Group. Baton Rouge, LA: *Advocate*, February 21: 7B.

Ravetz, Jerome R. 1971. *Scientific Knowledge and Its Social Problems*. Oxford: Clarendon Press.

Readings, Bill. 1996. *The University in Ruins*. Cambridge, MA: Harvard University Press.

Reamer, Frederic G. 1993. *The Philosophical Foundations of Social Work*. New York: Columbia University Press.

———. 1992. "The Place of Empiricism in Social Work," Editorial, *Journal of Social Work Education*, Fall, 28: 257–259.

Reich, Michael and Eileen Gambrill, eds. 1997. *Social Work in the 21st Century*. Thousand Oaks, CA: Pine Forge Press.

Rieff, David. 1995. *Slaughterhouse: Bosnia and the Failure of the West*. New York: Simon and Schuster.

Romanyshyn, John M., ed. 1974. *Social Science and Social Welfare*. New York: Council on Social Work Education.

Rorty, Richard. 1998. *Achieving Our Country. Leftist Thought in Twentieth Century America*. Cambridge, MA: Harvard University Press.

———. 1989. *Contingency, Irony, and Solidarity*. Cambridge: Cambridge University.

———. 1979. *Philosophy and the Mirror of Nature*. Princeton, NJ: Princeton University Press.

Ryan, A. 1995. "The Women in the Cowshed," *The New York Review of Books*, XLII (8), May 11: 24–26.

Ryan, William. 1971. *Blaming the Victim*. New York: Vintage Books.

Sachs, Jeffrey. 1998. "The Real Causes of Famine," *Time*, October 26: 69.

Sanders, Bernie. 1998. "Taxpayers Should Not Foot Bill for More IMF," Special to *Newsday*. Baton Rouge, LA: *Sunday Advocate*, September 27: 15B.

Sartre, Jean Paul. 1992. *Truth and Existence*. Chicago: The University of Chicago Press.

———. 1966–1976. *Critique of Dialectical Reason*. trans. A. Sheridan-Smith. London: New Left Books.

———. [1974] 1983. *Between Existentialism and Marxism*. trans. John Mathews. New York: Pantheon Books.

———. [1953] 1966. *Being and Nothingness: An Essay on Phenomenological Ontology*, trans. Hazel E. Barnes. New York: Washington Square Press.

Schram, Sanford F. 1995. *Words of Welfare: The Poverty of Social Science and the Social Science of Poverty*. Minneapolis: The University of Minnesota Press.

Schuerman, J. 1982. "Debate with Authors: The Obsolete Scientific Imperative in Social Work." *Social Service Review*, 56, 1: 144–146.

Searle, John R. 1977. "Consciousness and the Philosophers," *The New York Review of Books*, XLIV, March 6, 4: 43–50.

Segal, S. 1972. "Research on the Outcome of Social Work Therapeutic Interventions: A Review of the Literature." *Journal of Health and Social Behavior*, 13: 3–17.

Sen, Amartya. 1992. *Inequality Re-examined*. Cambridge, MA: Harvard University Press.

Serres, Michel. 1997. "Science and the Humanities: The Case of Turner," *The Journal of International Institute*. Ann Arbor: University of Michigan.

Sharma, Anupama. 1997. Personal communication.

Smolowe, Jill. 1995. "Making the Tough Calls," *Time*, December 11: 40–44.

Sniffen, Michael J. 1996. "Church Fires as Single Acts Seen as More Sinister than Conspiracy." Baton Rouge, LA: *Sunday Advocate*, June 23: 10A.

Sober, Elliott and David S. Wilson, 1998. *Unto Others: The Evolution and Psychology of Unselfish Behavior*. Cambridge, MA: Harvard University Press.

Spaeth, Anthony. 1995. "Engineer of Doom," *Time*, June 12: 57.

Specht, Harry. 1990. "Social Work and the Popular Psychotherapies." *Social service Review*, September, 345–357.

Specht, Harry and M. Courtney, 1994. *Unfaithful Angels*. New York: The Free Press.

Stanovich, Keith E. 1994. "Reconceptualizing Intelligence: Dysrationalia as an Intuition Pump," *Educational Researcher*, May, 11–22.

Steele, Shelby. 1995. "How Liberals Lost Their Virtue over Race," *Newsweek*, January 9: 41–42.

———. 1992. "The New Sovereignty," *Harper's*, July, 285, 1706: 47–54.

Stern, Fritz. 1989. *Dreams and Delusions*. New York: Vintage Books.

Stoesz, David. 1997. "The End of Social Work," in M. Reich and E. Gambrill (1997: 369–375).

Taft, John. 1989. *American Power: The Rise and Decline of U.S. Globalism*. New York: Harper & Row.

Tagore, Rabindranath. [1941] 1993. *Collected Poems and Plays*. New York: Collier Books.

Thurow, Lester. 1996. *The Future of Capitalism*. New York: William Morrow.

Time. 1996. "Russia Back to USSR?" May 27.

———. 1996a. "America's 25 Most Influential People." June 17: 52–77.

———. 1995. "A Shameful Death," December 11, cover.

———. 1995a. "Tough Talk on Entertainment," Forum, June 12: 32–35.

———. 1995b. June 19: 66.

———. 1994. "An American Tragedy," June 27 (Cover).

Toffler, Alvin. 1980. *The Third Wave*. New York: William Morrow & Co.

Toffler, A. and H. Toffler. 1993. *War and Anti-War: Survival at the Dawn of the Twenty-first Century*. New York: Little, Brown.

Tolstoy, Leo. 1995. *My Confessions*. London: Fount Paperback.

Turner, Francis J. 1997. "Social Work Practice: Theoretical Base," in Richard L. Edwards, ed. *Encyclopedia of Social Work*. Washington, D.C.: NASW Press.

————, ed. 1986. *Social Work Treatment: Interlocking Theoretical Perspective*. New York: Free Press.

Tyson, Katherine B. 1992. "A New Approach to Relevant Scientific Research to Practitioners: The Heuristic Paradigm," *Social Work*, 37, 6: 541–556.

Tyson, Remer. 1996. "Report Paints Dark Picture of Africa in Wake of AIDS." Baton Rouge, LA: *Sunday Advocate*, May 26: 1D.

United Nations. 1995. *Women in a Changing World Economy: 1994 World Survey on the Role of Women in Development*. New York: United Nations Publications.

————. 1995a. *World Submit for Social Development* (Social Summit Issue Papers), DPI/1619/A/SOC/CON–95.93103, January. New York: United Nations Department of Publications.

UNRISD. 1998. *States of Disarray: The Social Effects of Globalization*. Geneva: United Nations Research Institute for Social Development.

Wachtel, Paul L. 1989. *The Poverty of Affluence: A Psychological Portrait of the American Way of Life*. Santa Cruz, CA: New Society Publishers.

Wakefield, J. C. 1995. "When an Irresistible Epistemology Meets an Immovable Ontology." *Social Work Research*, 19, 1: 9–17.

————. 1993. "Psychoanalytic Fallacies: Reflections on Martha Heineman Pieper and William Joseph Pieper's Intrapsychic Humanism." *Social Service Review*, 67, 1: 127–155.

Weick, Ann. 1987. "Reconceptualizing the Conceptual Perspective of Social Work," *Social Service Review*, 61: 218–230.

Weinberg, Steven. 1998. "The Revolution That Didn't Happen." *The New York Review of Books*, 8 October, XLV, 15: 48–52.

Westbrook, Robert B. 1991. *John Dewey and American Democracy*. Ithaca, NY: Cornell University Press.

White, Barbara W. 1998. "Looking to the Roads Ahead." *Social Work Education Reporter*, Fall, 46, 3: 1.

Whitehead, Alfred N. 1961. *The Interpretation of Science: Selected Essays*. ed. A. H. Johnson, Johnson, NY: The Bobbs-Merrill Co.

Wideman, John E. 1995. "Tough Talk on Entertainment," Forum, *Time*, June 12: 33.

Wiesel, Elie. 1990. *From the Kingdom of Memory*. New York: Schocken Books.

Wills, Garry. 1995. "It's Just Another Way of Lying," Universal Press Syndicate. Baton Rouge, LA: *Sunday Advocate*, May 13: 6B.

Wilson, Edward O. 1998. *Consilience: The Unity of Knowledge*. New York: Knopf.

Wooten, B. 1959. *Social Science and Social Pathology*. London: George Allen and Unwin.

Wright, Lesley and Marti Smye. 1996. *Corporate Abuse*. New York: Macmillan.

Zarakhovich, Yuri. 1998. "A Russian's Lament," *Time*, September 21: 76.

Author Index

Subject Index

About the Author

BRIJ MOHAN is Professor of Social Work and former Dean at Louisiana State University School of Social Work. Professor Mohan is an internationally recognized scholar whose latest works include a trilogy on global development and human oppression published by Praeger (1992, 1993, and 1996). He is the founding editor-in-chief of *New Global Development: Journal of International & Comparative Social Work*.

ISBN 0-275-96114-1

HARDCOVER BAR CODE